Mastering
Minimal APIs in ASP.NET Core

Build, test, and prototype web APIs quickly using .NET and C#

Andrea Tosato

Marco Minerva

Emanuele Bartolesi

BIRMINGHAM—MUMBAI

Mastering Minimal APIs in ASP.NET Core

Group Product Manager: Pavan Ramchandani
Publishing Product Manager: Aaron Tanna
Senior Editor: Mark D'Souza
Senior Content Development Editor: Rakhi Patel
Technical Editor: Simran Ali
Copy Editor: Safis Editing
Project Coordinator: Sonam Pandey
Proofreader: Safis Editing
Indexer: Manju Arasan
Production Designer: Prashant Ghare
Marketing Coordinators: Anamika Singh and Marylou De Mello

First published: October 2022
Production reference: 1230922

Published by Packt Publishing Ltd.
Livery Place
35 Livery Street
Birmingham
B3 2PB, UK.

ISBN 978-1-80323-782-4

www.packt.com

In memory of my mother and father, Giovanna and Francesco, for their sacrifices and for supporting me in studying and facing new challenges every day.

– Andrea Tosato

To my family, friends, and colleagues, who have always believed in me during this journey.

– Marco Minerva

In memory of my beloved mom, and to my wife, Francesca, for her sacrifices and understanding.

Last but not least, to my son, Leonardo. The greatest success in my life.

– Emanuele Bartolesi

Contributors

About the authors

Andrea Tosato is a full stack software engineer and architect of .NET applications. Andrea has successfully developed .NET applications in various industries, sometimes facing complex technological challenges. He deals with desktop, web, and mobile development but with the arrival of the cloud, Azure has become his passion. In 2017, he co-founded Cloudgen Verona (a .NET community based in Verona, Italy) with his friend, Marco Zamana. In 2019, he was named Microsoft MVP for the first time in the Azure category. Andrea graduated from the University of Pavia with a degree in computer engineering in 2008 and successfully completed his master's degree, also in computer engineering, in Modena in 2011. Andrea was born in 1986 in Verona, Italy, where he currently works as a remote worker. You can find Andrea on Twitter.

Marco Minerva has been a computer enthusiast since elementary school when he received an old Commodore VIC-20 as a gift. He began developing with GW-BASIC. After some experience with Visual Basic, he has been using .NET since its first introduction. He got his master's degree in information technology in 2006. Today, he lives in Taggia, Italy, where he works as a freelance consultant and is involved in designing and developing solutions for the Microsoft ecosystem, building applications for desktop, mobile, and web. His expertise is in backend development as a software architect. He runs training courses, is a speaker at technical events, writes articles for magazines, and regularly makes live streams about coding on Twitch. He has been a Microsoft MVP since 2013. You can find Marco on Twitter.

Emanuele Bartolesi is a Microsoft 365 architect who is passionate about frontend technologies and everything related to the cloud, especially Microsoft Azure. He currently lives in Zurich and actively participates in local and international community activities and events. Emanuele shares his love of technology through his blog. He has also become a Twitch affiliate as a live coder, and you can find him as kasuken on Twitch to write some code with him. Emanuele has been a Microsoft MVP in the developer technologies category since 2014, and a GitHub Star since 2022. You can find Emanuele on Twitter.

About the reviewers

Marco Parenzan is a senior solution architect for Smart Factory, IoT, and Azure-based solutions at beanTech, a tech company in Italy. He has been a Microsoft Azure MVP since 2014 and has been playing with the cloud since 2010. He speaks about Azure and .NET development at major community events in Italy. He is a community lead for 1nn0va, a recognized Microsoft-oriented community in Pordenone, Italy, where he organizes local community events. He wrote a book on Azure for Packt Publishing in 2016. He loves playing with his Commodore 64 and trying to write small retro games in .NET or JavaScript.

Marco Zamana lives in Verona in the magnificent hills of Valpolicella. He has a background as a software developer and architect. He was Microsoft's Most Valuable Professional for 3 years in the artificial intelligence category. He currently works as a cloud solution architect in engineering at Microsoft. He is the co-founder of Cloudgen Verona, a Veronese association that discusses topics related to the cloud and, above all, Azure.

Ashirwad Satapathi works as an associate consultant at Microsoft and has expertise in building scalable applications with ASP.NET Core and Microsoft Azure. He is a published author and an active blogger in the C# Corner developer community. He was awarded the title of C# Corner **Most Valuable Professional (MVP)** in September 2020 and September 2021 for his contributions to the developer community. He is also a member of the Outreach Committee of the .NET Foundation.

Table of Contents

6

Exploring Validation and Mapping   119

7

Integration with the Data Access Layer   135

Part 3: Advanced Development and Microservices Concepts

8

Adding Authentication and Authorization   153

Preface

The simplification of code is every developer's dream. Minimal APIs are a new feature in .NET 6 that aims to simplify code. They are used for building APIs with minimal dependencies in ASP.NET Core. Minimal APIs simplify API development through the use of more compact code syntax.

Developers using minimal APIs will be able to take advantage of this syntax on some occasions to work more quickly with less code and fewer files to maintain. Here, you will be introduced to the main new features of .NET 6 and understand the basic themes of minimal APIs, which weren't available in .NET 5 and previous versions. You'll see how to enable Swagger for API documentation, along with CORS, and how to handle application errors. You will learn to structure your code better with Microsoft's new .NET framework called Dependency Injection. Finally, you will see the performance and benchmarking improvements in .NET 6 that are introduced with minimal APIs.

By the end of this book, you will be able to leverage minimal APIs and understand in what way they are related to the classic development of web APIs.

Who this book is for

This book is for .NET developers who want to build .NET and .NET Core APIs and want to study the new features of .NET 6. Basic knowledge of C#, .NET, Visual Studio, and REST APIs is assumed.

What this book covers

Chapter 1, *Introduction to Minimal APIs*, introduces you to the motivations behind introducing minimal APIs within .NET 6. We will explain the main new features of .NET 6 and the work that the .NET team is doing with this latest version. You will come to understand the reasons why we decided to write the book.

Chapter 2, *Exploring Minimal APIs and Their Advantages*, introduces you to the basic ways in which minimal APIs differ from .NET 5 and all previous versions. We will explore in detail routing and serialization with System.Text.JSON. Finally, we will end with some concepts related to writing our first REST API.

Chapter 3, *Working with Minimal APIs*, introduces you to the advanced ways in which minimal APIs differ from .NET 5 and all previous versions. We will explore in detail how to enable Swagger for API documentation. We will see how to enable CORS and how to handle application errors.

Chapter 4, *Dependency Injection in a Minimal API Project*, introduces you to Dependency Injection and goes over how to use it with a minimal API.

Chapter 5, Using Logging to Identify Errors, teaches you about the logging tools that .NET provides. A logger is one of the tools that developers have to use to debug an application or understand its failure in production. The logging library has been built into ASP.NET with several features enabled by design.

Chapter 6, Exploring Validation and Mapping, will teach you how to validate incoming data to an API and how to return any errors or messages. Once the data is validated, it can be mapped to a model that will then be used to process the request.

Chapter 7, Integration with the Data Access Layer, helps you understand the best practices for accessing and using data in minimal APIs.

Chapter 8, Adding Authentication and Authorization, looks at how to write an authentication and authorization system by leveraging our own database or a cloud service such as Azure Active Directory.

Chapter 9, Leveraging Globalization and Localization, shows you how to leverage the translation system in a minimal API project and provide errors in the same language of the client.

Chapter 10, Evaluating and Benchmarking the Performance of Minimal APIs, shows the improvements in .NET 6 and those that will be introduced with the minimal APIs.

To get the most out of this book

You will need Visual Studio 2022 with ASP.NET and a web development workload or Visual Studio Code and K6 installed on your computer.

All code examples have been tested using Visual Studio 2022 and Visual Studio Code on the Windows OS.

Software/hardware covered in the book	Operating system requirements
Visual Studio 2022	Windows, macOS, or Linux
Visual Studio Code	Windows, macOS, or Linux
K6 (ver 0.39)	Windows

If you are using the digital version of this book, we advise you to type the code yourself or access the code from the book's GitHub repository (a link is available in the next section). Doing so will help you avoid any potential errors related to the copying and pasting of code.

Basic development skills for Microsoft web technology are required to fully understand this book.

Download the example code files

You can download the example code files for this book from GitHub at `https://github.com/PacktPublishing/Minimal-APIs-in-ASP.NET-Core-6`. If there's an update to the code, it will be updated in the GitHub repository.

We also have other code bundles from our rich catalog of books and videos available at `https://github.com/PacktPublishing/`. Check them out!

Download the color images

We also provide a PDF file that has color images of the screenshots and diagrams used in this book.

You can download it here: `https://packt.link/GmUNL`

Conventions used

There are a number of text conventions used throughout this book.

`Code in text`: Indicates code words in text, database table names, folder names, filenames, file extensions, pathnames, dummy URLs, user input, and Twitter handles. Here is an example: "In minimal APIs, we define the route patterns using the `Map*` methods of the `WebApplication` object."

A block of code is set as follows:

```
app.MapGet("/hello-get", () => "[GET] Hello World!");
app.MapPost("/hello-post", () => "[POST] Hello World!");
app.MapPut("/hello-put", () => "[PUT] Hello World!");
app.MapDelete("/hello-delete", () => "[DELETE] Hello World!");
```

When we wish to draw your attention to a particular part of a code block, the relevant lines or items are set in bold:

```
if (app.Environment.IsDevelopment())
{
    app.UseSwagger();
    app.UseSwaggerUI();
}
```

Any command-line input or output is written as follows:

```
dotnet new webapi -minimal -o Chapter01
```

Bold: Indicates a new term, an important word, or words that you see onscreen. For instance, words in menus or dialog boxes appear in **bold**. Here is an example: "Open Visual Studio 2022 and from the main screen, click on **Create a new project**."

> **Tips or important notes**
> Appear like this.

Get in touch

Feedback from our readers is always welcome.

General feedback: If you have questions about any aspect of this book, email us at customercare@ packtpub.com and mention the book title in the subject of your message.

Errata: Although we have taken every care to ensure the accuracy of our content, mistakes do happen. If you have found a mistake in this book, we would be grateful if you would report this to us. Please visit www.packtpub.com/support/errata and fill in the form.

Piracy: If you come across any illegal copies of our works in any form on the internet, we would be grateful if you would provide us with the location address or website name. Please contact us at copyright@packt.com with a link to the material.

If you are interested in becoming an author: If there is a topic that you have expertise in and you are interested in either writing or contributing to a book, please visit authors.packtpub.com.

Share Your Thoughts

Once you've read *Mastering Minimal APIs in ASP.NET Core*, we'd love to hear your thoughts! Scan the QR code below to go straight to the Amazon review page for this book and share your feedback.

https://packt.link/r/1803237821

Your review is important to us and the tech community and will help us make sure we're delivering excellent quality content.

Part 1:
Introduction

In the first part of the book, we want to introduce you to the context of the book. We will explain the basics of minimal APIs and how they work. We want to add, brick by brick, the knowledge needed to take advantage of all the power that minimal APIs can grant us.

We will cover the following chapters in this part:

- *Chapter 1, Introduction to Minimal APIs*
- *Chapter 2, Exploring Minimal APIs and Their Advantages*
- *Chapter 3, Working with Minimal APIs*

1
Introduction to Minimal APIs

In this chapter of the book, we will introduce some basic themes related to minimal APIs in .NET 6.0, showing how to set up a development environment for .NET 6 and more specifically for developing minimal APIs with ASP.NET Core.

We will first begin with a brief history of minimal APIs. Then, we will create a new minimal API project with Visual Studio 2022 and Visual Code Studio. At the end, we will take a look at the structure of our project.

By the end of this chapter, you will be able to create a new minimal API project and start to work with this new template for a REST API.

In this chapter, we will be covering the following topics:

- A brief history of the Microsoft Web API
- Creating a new minimal API project
- Looking at the structure of the project

Technical requirements

To work with the ASP.NET Core 6 minimal APIs you need to install, first of all, .NET 6 on your development environment.

If you have not already installed it, let's do that now:

1. Navigate to the following link: `https://dotnet.microsoft.com`.
2. Click on the **Download** button.
3. By default, the browser chooses the right operating system for you, but if not, select your operating system at the top of the page.
4. Download the LTS version of the .NET 6.0 SDK.

5. Start the installer.

6. Reboot the machine (this is not mandatory).

You can see which SDKs are installed on your development machine using the following command in a terminal:

```
dotnet -list-sdks
```

Before you start coding, you will need a code editor or an **Integrated Development Environment (IDE)**. You can choose your favorite from the following list:

*   Visual Studio Code for Windows, Mac, or Linux

*   Visual Studio 2022

*   Visual Studio 2022 for Mac

In the last few years, Visual Studio Code has become very popular not only in the developer community but also in the Microsoft community. Even if you use Visual Studio 2022 for your day-to-day work, we recommend downloading and installing Visual Studio Code and giving it a try.

Let's download and install Visual Studio Code and some extensions:

1. Navigate to `https://code.visualstudio.com`.

2. Download the **Stable** or the **Insiders** edition.

3. Start the installer.

4. Launch Visual Studio Code.

5. Click on the **Extensions** icon.

    You will see the C# extension at the top of the list.

6. Click on the **Install** button and wait.

You can install other recommended extensions for developing with C# and ASP.NET Core. If you want to install them, you see our recommendations in the following table:

Extension name	Description
MSBuild project tools	Provides IntelliSense for MSBuild project files
REST Client	Sends an HTTP request and views the response directly in Visual Studio Code
ILSpy .NET Decompiler	Decompiles MSIL assemblies

Additionally, if you want to proceed with the IDE that's most widely used by .NET developers, you can download and install Visual Studio 2022.

If you don't have a license, check if you can use the Community Edition. There are a few restrictions on getting a license, but you can use it if you are a student, have open source projects, or want to use it as an individual. Here's how to download and install Visual Studio 2022:

1. Navigate to `https://visualstudio.microsoft.com/downloads/`.

2. Select Visual Studio 2022 version 17.0 or later and download it.

3. Start the installer.

4. On the **Workloads** tab, select the following:

   - **ASP.NET and web development**

   - **Azure Development**

5. On the **Individual Components** tab, select the following:

   - **Git for Windows**

All the code samples in this chapter can be found in the GitHub repository for this book at `https://github.com/PacktPublishing/Minimal-APIs-in-ASP.NET-Core-6/tree/main/Chapter01`.

Now, you have an environment in which you can follow and try the code used in this book.

A brief history of the Microsoft Web API

A few years ago in 2007, .NET web applications went through an evolution with the introduction of ASP.NET MVC. Since then, .NET has provided native support for the Model-View-Controller pattern that was common in other languages.

Five years later, in 2012, RESTful APIs were the new trend on the internet and .NET responded to this with a new approach for developing APIs, called ASP.NET Web API. It was a significant improvement over **Windows Communication Foundation** (**WCF**) because it was easier to develop services for the web. Later, in ASP.NET Core these frameworks were unified under the name ASP.NET Core MVC: one single framework with which to develop web applications and APIs.

In ASP.NET Core MVC applications, the controller is responsible for accepting inputs, orchestrating operations, and at the end, returning a response. A developer can extend the entire pipeline with filters, binding, validation, and much more. It's a fully featured framework for building modern web applications.

But in the real world, there are also scenarios and use cases where you don't need all the features of the MVC framework or you have to factor in a constraint on performance. ASP.NET Core implements a lot of middleware that you can remove from or add to your applications at will, but there are a lot of common features that you would need to implement by yourself in this scenario.

At last, ASP.NET Core 6.0 has filled these gaps with minimal APIs.

Now that we have covered a brief history of minimal APIs, we will start creating a new minimal API project in the next section.

Creating a new minimal API project

Let's start with our first project and try to analyze the new template for the minimal API approach when writing a RESTful API.

In this section, we will create our first minimal API project. We will start by using Visual Studio 2022 and then we will show how you can also create the project with Visual Studio Code and the .NET CLI.

Creating the project with Visual Studio 2022

Follow these steps to create a new project in Visual Studio 2022:

1. Open Visual Studio 2022 and on the main screen, click on **Create a new project**:

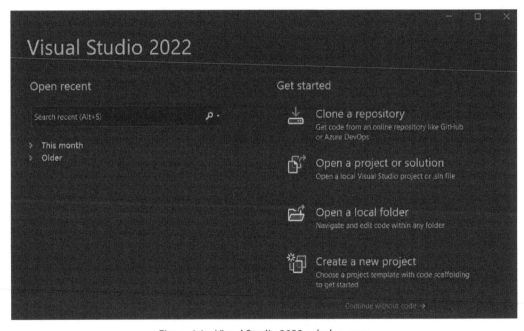

Figure 1.1 – Visual Studio 2022 splash screen

2. On the next screen, write API in the textbox at the top of the window and select the template called **ASP.NET Core Web API**:

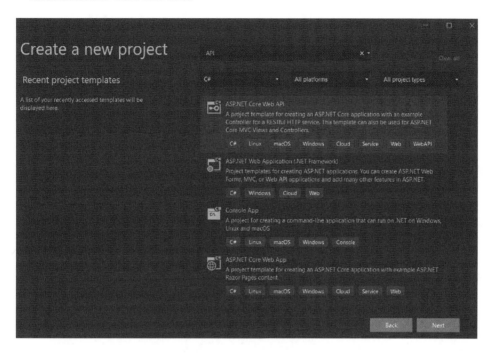

Figure 1.2 – Create a new project screen

3. Next, on the **Configure your new project** screen, insert a name for the new project and select the root folder for your new solution:

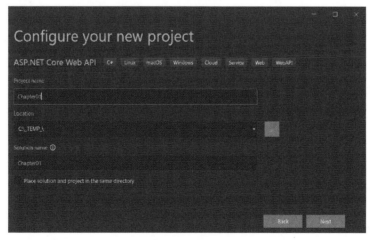

Figure 1.3 – Configure your new project screen

For this example we will use the name Chapter01, but you can choose any name that appeals to you.

4. On the following **Additional information** screen, make sure to select **.NET 6.0 (Long-term-support)** from the **Framework** dropdown. And most important of all, uncheck the **Use controllers (uncheck to use minimal APIs)** option.

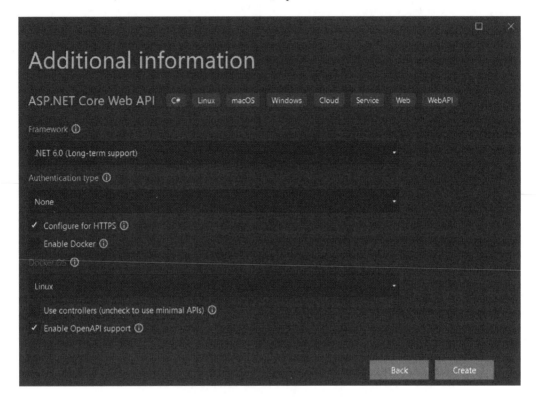

Figure 1.4 – Additional information screen

5. Click **Create** and, after a few seconds, you will see the code of your new minimal API project.

Now we are going to show how to create the same project using Visual Studio Code and the .NET CLI.

Creating the project with Visual Studio Code

Creating a project with Visual Studio Code is easier and faster than with Visual Studio 2022 because you don't have to use a UI or wizard, rather just a terminal and the .NET CLI.

You don't need to install anything new for this because the .NET CLI is included with the .NET 6 installation (as in the previous versions of the .NET SDKs). Follow these steps to create a project using Visual Studio Code:

1. Open your console, shell, or Bash terminal, and switch to your working directory.

2. Use the following command to create a new Web API application:

    ```
    dotnet new webapi -minimal -o Chapter01
    ```

    As you can see, we have inserted the `-minimal` parameter in the preceding command to use the minimal API project template instead of the ASP.NET Core template with the controllers.

3. Now open the new project with Visual Studio Code using the following commands:

    ```
    cd Chapter01
    code.
    ```

Now that we know how to create a new minimal API project, we are going to have a quick look at the structure of this new template.

Looking at the structure of the project

Whether you are using Visual Studio or Visual Studio Code, you should see the following code in the `Program.cs` file:

```
var builder = WebApplication.CreateBuilder(args);

// Add services to the container.
// Learn more about configuring Swagger/OpenAPI at https://aka.
ms/aspnetcore/swashbuckle
builder.Services.AddEndpointsApiExplorer();
builder.Services.AddSwaggerGen();

var app = builder.Build();

// Configure the HTTP request pipeline.
if (app.Environment.IsDevelopment())
{
    app.UseSwagger();
    app.UseSwaggerUI();
}
```

```
app.UseHttpsRedirection();

var summaries = new[]
{
    "Freezing", "Bracing", "Chilly", "Cool", "Mild", "Warm",
    "Balmy", "Hot", "Sweltering", "Scorching"
};

app.MapGet("/weatherforecast", () =>
{
  var forecast = Enumerable.Range(1, 5).Select(index =>
      new WeatherForecast
      (
          DateTime.Now.AddDays(index),
          Random.Shared.Next(-20, 55),
          summaries[Random.Shared.Next(summaries.Length)]
      ))
      .ToArray();
      return forecast;
})
.WithName("GetWeatherForecast");

app.Run();

internal record WeatherForecast(DateTime Date, int
TemperatureC, string? Summary)
{
    public int TemperatureF => 32 + (int)(TemperatureC /
    0.5556);
}
```

First of all, with the minimal API approach, all of your code will be inside the Program.cs file. If you are a seasoned .NET developer, it's easy to understand the preceding code, and you'll find it similar to some of the things you've always used with the controller approach.

At the end of the day, it's another way to write an API, but it's based on ASP.NET Core.

However, if you are new to ASP.NET, this single file approach is easy to understand. It's easy to understand how to extend the code in the template and add more features to this API.

Don't forget that minimal means that it contains the minimum set of components needed to build an HTTP API but it doesn't mean that the application you are going to build will be simple. It will require a good design like any other .NET application.

As a final point, the minimal API approach is not a replacement for the MVC approach. It's just another way to write the same thing.

Let's go back to the code.

Even the template of the minimal API uses the new approach of .NET 6 web applications: a top-level statement.

It means that the project has a `Program.cs` file only instead of using two files to configure an application.

If you don't like this style of coding, you can convert your application to the old template for ASP.NET Core 3.x/5. This approach still continues to work in .NET as well.

> **Important note**
>
> We can find more information about the `.NET 6 top-level statements` template at `https://docs.microsoft.com/dotnet/core/tutorials/top-level-templates`.

By default, the new template includes support for the OpenAPI Specification and more specifically, Swagger.

Let's say that we have our documentation and playground for the endpoints working out of the box without any additional configuration needed.

You can see the default configuration for Swagger in the following two lines of codes:

```
builder.Services.AddEndpointsApiExplorer();
builder.Services.AddSwaggerGen();
```

Very often, you don't want to expose Swagger and all the endpoints to the production or staging environments. The default template enables Swagger out of the box only in the development environment with the following lines of code:

```
if (app.Environment.IsDevelopment())
{
```

```
        app.UseSwagger();
        app.UseSwaggerUI();
}
```

If the application is running on the dev elopment environment, you must also include the Swagger documentation, but otherwise not.

> **Note**
>
> We'll talk in detail about Swagger in *Chapter 3, Working with Minimal APIs*.

In these last few lines of code in the template, we are introducing another generic concept for .NET 6 web applications: environments.

Typically, when we develop a professional application, there are a lot of phases through which an application is developed, tested, and finally published to the end users.

By convention, these phases are regulated and called development, staging, and production. As developers, we might like to change the behavior of the application based on the current environment.

There are several ways to access this information but the typical way to retrieve the actual environment in modern .NET 6 applications is to use environment variables. You can access the environment variables directly from the app variable in the Program.cs file.

The following code block shows how to retrieve all the information about the environments directly from the startup point of the application:

```
if (app.Environment.IsDevelopment())
{
        // your code here
}
if (app.Environment.IsStaging())
{
        // your code here
}
if (app.Environment.IsProduction())
{
        // your code here
}
```

In many cases, you can define additional environments, and you can check your custom environment with the following code:

```
if (app.Environment.IsEnvironment("TestEnvironment"))
{
        // your code here
}
```

To define routes and handlers in minimal APIs, we use the MapGet, MapPost, MapPut, and MapDelete methods. If you are used to using HTTP verbs, you will have noticed that the verb Patch is not present, but you can define any set of verbs using MapMethods.

For instance, if you want to create a new endpoint to post some data to the API, you can write the following code:

```
app.MapPost("/weatherforecast", async (WeatherForecast
    model, IWeatherService repo) =>
{
        // ...
});
```

As you can see in the short preceding code, it's very easy to add a new endpoint with the new minimal API template.

It was more difficult previously, especially for a new developer, to code a new endpoint with binding parameters and use dependency injection.

> **Important note**
> We'll talk in detail about routing in *Chapter 2, Exploring Minimal APIs and Their Advantages*, and about dependency injection in *Chapter 4, Dependency Injection in a Minimal API Project*.

Summary

In this chapter, we first started with a brief history of minimal APIs. Next, we saw how to create a project with Visual Studio 2022 as well as Visual Studio Code and the .NET CLI. After that, we examined the structure of the new template, how to access different environments, and how to start interacting with REST endpoints.

In the next chapter, we will see how to bind parameters, the new routing configuration, and how to customize a response.

2
Exploring Minimal APIs and Their Advantages

In this chapter of the book, we will introduce some of the basic themes related to minimal APIs in .NET 6.0, showing how they differ from the controller-based web APIs that we have written in the previous version of .NET. We will also try to underline both the pros and the cons of this new approach of writing APIs.

In this chapter, we will be covering the following topics:

- Routing
- Parameter binding
- Exploring responses
- Controlling serialization
- Architecting a minimal API project

Technical requirements

To follow the descriptions in this chapter, you will need to create an ASP.NET Core 6.0 Web API application. You can either use one of the following options:

- **Option 1**: Click on the **New | Project** command in the **File** menu of Visual Studio 2022 – then, choose the **ASP.NET Core Web API** template. Select a name and the working directory in the wizard and be sure to uncheck the **Use controllers (uncheck to use minimal APIs)** option in the next step.

- **Option 2**: Open your console, shell, or Bash terminal, and change to your working directory. Use the following command to create a new Web API application:

```
dotnet new webapi -minimal -o Chapter02
```

Now, open the project in Visual Studio by double-clicking the project file, or in Visual Studio Code, by typing the following command in the already open console:

```
cd Chapter02
code.
```

Finally, you can safely remove all the code related to the `WeatherForecast` sample, as we don't need it for this chapter.

All the code samples in this chapter can be found in the GitHub repository for this book at `https://github.com/PacktPublishing/Minimal-APIs-in-ASP.NET-Core-6/tree/main/Chapter02`.

Routing

According to the official Microsoft documentation available at `https://docs.microsoft.com/aspnet/core/fundamentals/routing`, the following definition is given for routing:

> *Routing is responsible for matching incoming HTTP requests and dispatching those requests to the app's executable endpoints. Endpoints are the app's units of executable request-handling code. Endpoints are defined in the app and configured when the app starts. The endpoint matching process can extract values from the request's URL and provide those values for request processing. Using endpoint information from the app, routing is also able to generate URLs that map to endpoints.*

In controller-based web APIs, routing is defined via the `UseEndpoints()` method in `Startup.cs` or using data annotations such as `Route`, `HttpGet`, `HttpPost`, `HttpPut`, `HttpPatch`, and `HttpDelete` right over the action methods.

As mentioned in *Chapter 1, Introduction to Minimal APIs* in minimal APIs, we define the route patterns using the `Map*` methods of the `WebApplication` object. Here's an example:

```
app.MapGet("/hello-get", () => "[GET] Hello World!");
app.MapPost("/hello-post", () => "[POST] Hello World!");
app.MapPut("/hello-put", () => "[PUT] Hello World!");
app.MapDelete("/hello-delete", () => "[DELETE] Hello
              World!");
```

In this code, we have defined four endpoints, each with a different routing and method. Of course, we can use the same route pattern with different HTTP verbs.

> **Note**
>
> As soon as we add an endpoint to our application (for example, using `MapGet()`), `UseRouting()` is automatically added at the start of the middleware pipeline and `UseEndpoints()` at the end of the pipeline.

As shown here, ASP.NET Core 6.0 provides `Map*` methods for the most common HTTP verbs. If we need to use other verbs, we can use the generic `MapMethods`:

```
app.MapMethods("/hello-patch", new[] { HttpMethods.Patch },
    () => "[PATCH] Hello World!");
app.MapMethods("/hello-head", new[] { HttpMethods.Head },
    () => "[HEAD] Hello World!");
app.MapMethods("/hello-options", new[] {
    HttpMethods.Options }, () => "[OPTIONS] Hello World!");
```

In the following sections, we will show in detail how routing works effectively and how we can control its behavior.

Route handlers

Methods that execute when a route URL matches (according to parameters and constraints, as described in the following sections) are called **route handlers**. Route handlers can be a lambda expression, a local function, an instance method, or a static method, whether synchronous or asynchronous:

- Here's an example of a lambda expression (inline or using a variable):

  ```
  app.MapGet("/hello-inline", () => "[INLINE LAMBDA]
              Hello World!");

  var handler = () => "[LAMBDA VARIABLE] Hello World!";
  app.MapGet("/hello", handler);
  ```

- Here's an example of a local function:

  ```
  string Hello() => "[LOCAL FUNCTION] Hello World!";
  app.MapGet("/hello", Hello);
  ```

- The following is an example of an instance method:

  ```
  var handler = new HelloHandler();
  app.MapGet("/hello", handler.Hello);
  ```

```
class HelloHandler
{
    public string Hello()
        => "[INSTANCE METHOD] Hello
            World!";
}
```

- Here, we can see an example of a static method:

```
app.MapGet("/hello", HelloHandler.Hello);

class HelloHandler
{
    public static string Hello()
        => "[STATIC METHOD] Hello World!";
}
```

Route parameters

As with the previous versions of .NET, we can create route patterns with parameters that will be automatically captured by the handler:

```
app.MapGet("/users/{username}/products/{productId}",
        (string username, int productId)
        => $"The Username is {username} and the product Id
            is {productId}");
```

A route can contain an arbitrary number of parameters. When a request is made to this route, the parameters will be captured, parsed, and passed as arguments to the corresponding handler. In this way, the handler will always receive typed arguments (in the preceding sample, we are sure that the username is `string` and the product ID is `int`).

If the route values cannot be casted to the specified types, then an exception of the `BadHttpRequestException` type will be thrown, and the API will respond with a `400 Bad Request` message.

Route constraints

Route constraints are used to restrict valid types for route parameters. Typical constraints allow us to specify that a parameter must be a number, a string, or a GUID. To specify a route constraint, we simply need to add a colon after the parameter name, then specify the constraint name:

```
app.MapGet("/users/{id:int}", (int id) => $"The user Id is
                                             {id}");
app.MapGet("/users/{id:guid}", (Guid id) => $"The user Guid
                                             is {id}");
```

Minimal APIs support all the route constraints that were already available in the previous versions of ASP.NET Core. You can find the full list of route constraints at the following link: https://docs. microsoft.com/aspnet/core/fundamentals/routing#route-constraint-reference.

If, according to the constraints, no route matches the specified path, we don't get an exception. Instead we obtain a 404 Not Found message, because, in fact, if the constraints do not fit, the route itself isn't reachable. So, for example, in the following cases we get 404 responses:

Route	Path
users/{id:int}	users/marco
users/{id:guid}	users/42

Table 2.1 – Examples of an invalid path according to the route constraints

Every other argument in the handler that is not declared as a route constraint is expected, by default, in the query string. For example, see the following:

```
// Matches hello?name=Marco
app.MapGet("/hello", (string name) => $"Hello, {name}!");
```

In the next section, *Parameter binding*, we'll go deeper into how to use binding to further customize routing by specifying, for example, where to search for routing arguments, how to change their names, and how to have optional route parameters.

Parameter binding

Parameter binding is the process that converts request data (i.e., URL paths, query strings, or the body) into strongly typed parameters that can be consumed by route handlers. ASP.NET Core minimal APIs support the following binding sources:

- Route values
- Query strings
- Headers
- The body (as JSON, the only format supported by default)
- A service provider (dependency injection)

    We'll talk in detail about dependency injection in *Chapter 4, Implementing Dependency Injection*.

As we'll see later in this chapter, if necessary, we can customize the way in which binding is performed for a particular input. Unfortunately, in the current version, binding from Form is not natively supported in minimal APIs. This means that, for example, IFormFile is not supported either.

To better understand how parameter binding works, let's take a look at the following API:

```
var builder = WebApplication.CreateBuilder(args);
builder.Services.AddScoped<PeopleService>();


var app = builder.Build();


app.MapPut("/people/{id:int}", (int id, bool notify, Person
            person, PeopleService peopleService) => { });


app.Run();


public class PeopleService { }


public record class Person(string FirstName, string
                          LastName);
```

Parameters that are passed to the handler are resolved in the following ways:

Parameter	Source
id	Route
Notify	Query string (case insensitive)
Person	Body (as JSON)
peopleService	Service provider

Table 2.2 – Parameter binding sources

As we can see, ASP.NET Core is able to automatically understand where to search for parameters for binding, based on the route pattern and the types of the parameters themselves. For example, a complex type such as the Person class is expected in the request body.

If needed, as in the previous versions of ASP.NET Core, we can use attributes to explicitly specify where parameters are bound from and, optionally, use different names for them. See the following endpoint:

```
app.MapGet("/search", string q) => { });
```

The API can be invoked with /search?q=text. However, using q as the name of the argument isn't a good idea, because its meaning is not self-explanatory. So, we can modify the handler using FromQueryAttribute:

```
app.MapGet("/search", ([FromQuery(Name = "q")] string
        searchText) => { });
```

In this way, the API still expects a query string parameter named q, but in the handler its value is now bound to the searchText argument.

> **Note**
>
> According to the standard, the GET, DELETE, HEAD, and OPTIONS HTTP options should never have a body. If, nevertheless, you want to use it, you need to explicitly add the [FromBody] attribute to the handler argument; otherwise, you'll get an InvalidOperationException error. However, keep in mind that this is a bad practice.

By default, all the parameters in route handlers are required. So, if, according to routing, ASP.NET Core finds a valid route, but not all the required parameters are provided, we will get an error. For example, let's look at the following method:

```
app.MapGet("/people", (int pageIndex, int itemsPerPage) => {
});
```

If we call the endpoint without the `pageIndex` or `itemsPerPage` query string values, we will obtain a `BadHttpRequestException` error, and the response will be `400 Bad Request`.

To make the parameters optional, we just need to declare them as nullable or provide a default value. The latter case is the most common. However, if we adopt this solution, we cannot use a lambda expression for the handler. We need another approach, for example, a local function:

```
// This won't compile
//app.MapGet("/people", (int pageIndex = 0, int
                        itemsPerPage = 50) => { });

string SearchMethod(int pageIndex = 0,
                    int itemsPerPage = 50) => $"Sample
                    result for page {pageIndex} getting
                    {itemsPerPage} elements";
app.MapGet("/people", SearchMethod);
```

In this case, we are dealing with a query string, but the same rules apply to all the binding sources.

Keep in mind that if we use **nullable reference types** (which are enabled by default in .NET 6.0 projects) and we have, for example, a string parameter that could be `null`, we need to declare it as **nullable** – otherwise, we'll get a `BadHttpRequestException` error again. The following example correctly defines the `orderBy` query string parameter as optional:

```
app.MapGet("/people", (string? orderBy) => $"Results ordered by
{orderBy}");
```

Special bindings

In controller-based web APIs, a controller that inherits from `Microsoft.AspNetCore.Mvc.ControllerBase` has access to some properties that allows it to get the context of the request and response: `HttpContext`, `Request`, `Response`, and `User`. In minimal APIs, we don't have a base class, but we can still access this information because it is treated as a special binding that is always available to any handler:

```
app.MapGet("/products", (HttpContext context, HttpRequest req,
HttpResponse res, ClaimsPrincipal user) => { });
```

> **Tip**
> We can also access all these objects using the `IHttpContextAccessor` interface, as we did in the previous ASP.NET Core versions.

Custom binding

In some cases, the default way in which parameter binding works isn't enough for our purpose. In minimal APIs, we don't have support for the IModelBinderProvider and IModelBinder interfaces, but we have two alternatives to implement custom model binding.

> **Important note**
>
> The IModelBinderProvider and IModelBinder interfaces in controller-based projects allow us to define the mapping between the request data and the application model. The default model binder provided by ASP.NET Core supports most of the common data types, but, if necessary, we can extend the system by creating our own providers. We can find more information at the following link: https://docs.microsoft.com/aspnet/core/mvc/advanced/custom-model-binding.

If we want to bind a parameter that comes from a route, query string, or header to a custom type, we can add a static TryParse method to the type:

```
// GET /navigate?location=43.8427,7.8527
app.MapGet("/navigate", (Location location) => $"Location:
            {location.Latitude}, {location.Longitude}");


public class Location
{
    public double Latitude { get; set; }

    public double Longitude { get; set; }

    public static bool TryParse(string? value,
       IFormatProvider? provider, out Location? location)
    {
        if (!string.IsNullOrWhiteSpace(value))
        {
            var values = value.Split(',',
            StringSplitOptions.RemoveEmptyEntries);

            if (values.Length == 2 && double.
               TryParse(values[0],
               NumberStyles.AllowDecimalPoint,
```

```
                    CultureInfo.InvariantCulture,
                    out var latitude) && double.
                    TryParse(values[1], NumberStyles.
                    AllowDecimalPoint, CultureInfo.
                    InvariantCulture, out var longitude))
            {
                    location = new Location
                    { Latitude = latitude,
                    Longitude = longitude };
                    return true;
            }
        }

        location = null;
        return false;
    }
}
```

In the `TryParse` method, we can try to split the input parameter and check whether it contains two decimal values: in this case, we parse the numbers to build the `Location` object and we return `true`. Otherwise, we return `false` because the `Location` object cannot be initialized.

> **Important note**
>
> When the minimal API finds that a type contains a static `TryParse` method, even if it is a complex type, it assumes that it is passed in the route or the query string, based on the routing template. We can use the `[FromHeader]` attributes to change the binding source. In any case, `TryParse` will never be invoked for the body of the request.

If we need to completely control how binding is performed, we can implement a static `BindAsync` method on the type. This isn't a very common solution, but in some cases, it can be useful:

```
// POST /navigate?lat=43.8427&lon=7.8527
app.MapPost("/navigate", (Location location) =>
    $"Location: {location.Latitude}, {location.Longitude}");


public class Location
{
    // ...
```

```
public static ValueTask<Location?> BindAsync(HttpContext
context, ParameterInfo parameter)
{
    if (double.TryParse(context.Request.Query["lat"],
        NumberStyles.AllowDecimalPoint, CultureInfo.
        InvariantCulture, out var latitude)&& double.
        TryParse(context.Request.Query["lon"],
        NumberStyles.AllowDecimalPoint, CultureInfo.
        InvariantCulture, out var longitude))
    {

        var location = new Location
        { Latitude = latitude, Longitude = longitude };
        return ValueTask.
            FromResult<Location?>(location);

    }

    return ValueTask.FromResult<Location?>(null);
}
}
```

As we can see, the BindAsync method takes the whole HttpContext as an argument, so we can read all the information we need to create the actual Location object that is passed to the route handler. In this example, we read two query string parameters (lat and lon), but (in the case of POST, PUT, or PATCH methods) we can also read the entire body of the request and manually parse its content. This can be useful, for instance, if we need to handle requests that have a format other than JSON (which, as said before, is the only one supported by default).

If the BindAsync method returns null, while the corresponding route handler parameter cannot assume this value (as in the previous example), we will get an HttpBadRequestException error, which. as usual, will be wrapped in a 400 Bad Request response.

> **Important note**
> We shouldn't define both the TryParse and BindAsync methods using a type; if both are present, BindAsync always has precedence (that is, TryParse will never be invoked).

Now that we have looked at parameter binding and understood how to use it and customize its behavior, let's see how to work with responses in minimal APIs.

Exploring responses

As with controller-based projects, with route handlers of minimal APIs as well, we can directly return a string or a class (either synchronously or asynchronously):

- If we return a string (as in the examples of the previous section), the framework writes the string directly to the response, setting its content type to text/plain and the status code to 200 OK

- If we use a class, the object is serialized into the JSON format and sent to the response with the application/json content type and a 200 OK status code

However, in a real application, we typically need to control the response type and the status code. In this case, we can use the static Results class, which allows us to return an instance of the IResult interface, which in minimal APIs acts how IActionResult does for controllers. For instance, we can use it to return a 201 Created response rather than a 400 Bad Request or a 404 Not Found message. L et's look at some examples:

```
app.MapGet("/ok", () => Results.Ok(new Person("Donald",
                                               "Duck")));


app.MapGet("/notfound", () => Results.NotFound());


app.MapPost("/badrequest", () =>
{
    // Creates a 400 response with a JSON body.
    return Results.BadRequest(new { ErrorMessage = "Unable to
                                    complete the request" });
});


app.MapGet("/download", (string fileName) =>
        Results.File(fileName));


record class Person(string FirstName, string LastName);
```

Each method of the Results class is responsible for setting the response type and status code that correspond to the meaning of the method itself (e.g., the Results.NotFound() method returns a 404 Not Found response). Note that even if we typically need to return an object in the case of a 200 OK response (with Results.Ok()), it isn't the only method that allows this. Many other methods allow us to include a custom response; in all these cases, the response type will be set to application/json and the object will automatically be JSON-serialized.

The current version of minimal APIs does not support content negotiation. We only have a few methods that allow us to explicitly set the content type, when getting a file with `Results.Bytes()`, `Results.Stream()`, and `Results.File()`, or when using `Results.Text()` and `Results.Content()`. In all other cases, when we're dealing with complex objects, the response will be in JSON format. This is a precise design choice since most developers rarely need to support other media types. By supporting only JSON without performing content negotiation, minimal APIs can be very efficient.

However, this approach isn't enough in all scenarios. In some cases, we may need to create a custom response type, for example, if we want to return an HTML or XML response instead of the standard JSON. We can manually use the `Results.Content()` method (which allows us to specify the content as a simple string with a particular content type), but, if we have this requirement, it is better to implement a custom `IResult` type, so that the solution can be reused.

For example, let's suppose that we want to serialize objects in XML instead of JSON. We can then define an `XmlResult` class that implements the `IResult` interface:

```
public class XmlResult : IResult
{
    private readonly object value;

    public XmlResult(object value)
    {
        this.value = value;
    }

    public Task ExecuteAsync(HttpContext httpContext)
    {
        using var writer = new StringWriter();

        var serializer = new XmlSerializer(value.GetType());
        serializer.Serialize(writer, value);

        var xml = writer.ToString();
        httpContext.Response.ContentType = MediaTypeNames.
        Application.Xml;
        httpContext.Response.ContentLength = Encoding.UTF8
        .GetByteCount(xml);

        return httpContext.Response.WriteAsync(xml);
```

```
        }
    }
```

The `IResult` interface requires us to implement the `ExecuteAsync` method, which receives the current `HttpContext` as an argument. We serialize the value using the `XmlSerializer` class and then write it to the response, specifying the correct response type.

Now, we can directly use the new `XmlResult` type in our route handlers. However, best practices suggest that we create an extension method for the `IResultExtensions` interface, as with the following one:

```
public static class ResultExtensions
{
    public static IResult Xml(this IResultExtensions
    resultExtensions, object value) => new XmlResult(value);
}
```

In this way, we have a new `Xml` method available on the `Results.Extensions` property:

```
app.MapGet("/xml", () => Results.Extensions.Xml(new City { Name
= "Taggia" }));

public record class City
{
    public string? Name { get; init; }
}
```

The benefit of this approach is that we can reuse it everywhere we need to deal with XML without having to manually handle the serialization and the response type (as we should have done using the `Result.Content()` method instead).

Tip

If we want to perform content validation, we need to manually check the `Accept` header of the `HttpRequest` object, which we can pass to our handlers, and then create the correct response accordingly.

After analyzing how to properly handle responses in minimal APIs, we'll see how to control the way our data is serialized and deserialized in the next section.

Controlling serialization

As described in the previous sections, minimal APIs only provide built-in support for the JSON format. In particular, the framework uses `System.Text.Json` for serialization and deserialization. In controller-based APIs, we can change this default and use JSON.NET instead. This is not possible when working with minimal APIs: we can't replace the serializer at all.

The built-in serializer uses the following options:

- Case-insensitive property names during serialization

- Camel case property naming policy

- Support for quoted numbers (JSON strings for number properties)

> **Note**
>
> We can find more information about the `System.Text.Json` namespace and all the APIs it provides at the following link: `https://docs.microsoft.com/dotnet/api/system.text.json`.

In controller-based APIs, we can customize these settings by calling `AddJsonOptions()` fluently after `AddControllers()`. In minimal APIs, we can't use this approach since we don't have controllers at all, so we need to explicitly call the `Configure` method for `JsonOptions`. So, let's consider this handler:

```
app.MapGet("/product", () =>
{
    var product = new Product("Apple", null, 0.42, 6);
    return Results.Ok(product);
});
public record class Product(string Name, string? Description,
double UnitPrice, int Quantity)
{
    public double TotalPrice => UnitPrice * Quantity;
}
```

Using the default JSON options, we get this result:

```
{
    "name": "Apple",
    "description": null,
    "unitPrice": 0.42,
```

```
    "quantity": 6,
    "totalPrice": 2.52
}
```

Now, let's configure JsonOptions:

```
var builder = WebApplication.CreateBuilder(args);

builder.Services.Configure<Microsoft.AspNetCore.Http.Json.
JsonOptions>(options =>
{
    options.SerializerOptions.DefaultIgnoreCondition =
    JsonIgnoreCondition.WhenWritingNull;
    options.SerializerOptions.IgnoreReadOnlyProperties
    = true;
});
```

Calling the /product endpoint again, we'll now get the following:

```
{
    "name": "Apple",
    "unitPrice": 0.42,
    "quantity": 6
}
```

As expected, the Description property hasn't been serialized because it is null, as well as TotalPrice, which isn't included in the response because it is read-only.

Another typical use case for JsonOptions is when we want to add converters that will be automatically applied for each serialization or deserialization, for example, JsonStrinEnumConverter to convert enumeration values into or from strings.

> **Important note**
>
> Be aware that the JsonOptions class used by minimal APIs is the one available in the Microsoft.AspNetCore.Http.Json namespace. Do not confuse it with the one that is defined in the Microsoft.AspNetCore.Mvc namespace; the name of the object is the same, but the latter is valid only for controllers, so it has no effect if set in a minimal API project.

Because of the JSON-only support, if we do not explicitly add support for other formats, as described in the previous sections (using, for example, the `BindAsync` method on a custom type), minimal APIs will automatically perform some validations on the body binding source and handle the following scenarios:

Problem	Response status code
Content type not set to `application/json`	415
Unable to read the body as JSON	400

Table 2.3 – The response status codes for body binding problems

In these cases, because body validation fails, our route handlers will never be invoked, and we will get the response status codes shown in the preceding table directly.

Now, we have covered all the pillars that we need to start developing minimal APIs. However, there is another important thing to talk about: the correct way to design a real project to avoid common mistakes within the architecture.

Architecting a minimal API project

Up to now, we have written route handlers directly in the `Program.cs` file. This is a perfectly supported scenario: with minimal APIs, we can write all our code inside this single file. In fact, almost all the samples show this solution. However, while this is allowed, we can easily imagine how this approach can lead to unstructured and therefore unmaintainable projects. If we have fewer endpoints, it is fine – otherwise, it is better to organize our handlers in separate files.

Let's suppose that we have the following code right in the `Program.cs` file because we have to handle CRUD operations:

```
app.MapGet("/api/people", (PeopleService peopleService) =>
            { });
app.MapGet("/api/people/{id:guid}", (Guid id, PeopleService
            peopleService) => { });
app.MapPost("/api/people", (Person Person, PeopleService
            people) => { });

app.MapPut("/api/people/{id:guid}", (Guid id, Person
            Person, PeopleService people) => { });
```

```
app.MapDelete("/api/people/{id:guid}", (Guid id,
                PeopleService people) => { });
```

It's easy to imagine that, if we have all the implementation here (even if we're using `PeopleService` to extract the business logic), this file can easily explode. So, in real scenarios, the inline lambda approach isn't the best practice. We should use the other methods that we have covered in the *Routing* section to define the handlers instead. So, it is a good idea to create an external class to hold all the route handlers:

```
public class PeopleHandler
{
    public static void MapEndpoints(IEndpointRouteBuilder
    app)
    {
        app.MapGet("/api/people", GetList);
        app.MapGet("/api/people/{id:guid}", Get);
        app.MapPost("/api/people", Insert);
        app.MapPut("/api/people/{id:guid}", Update);
        app.MapDelete("/api/people/{id:guid}", Delete);
    }


    private static IResult GetList(PeopleService
    peopleService) { /* ... */ }

    private static IResult Get(Guid id, PeopleService
    peopleService) { /* ... */ }

    private static IResult Insert(Person person,
    PeopleService people) { /* ... */ }

    private static IResult Update(Guid id, Person
    person, PeopleService people) { /* ... */ }

    private static IResult Delete(Guid id) { /* ... */ }
}
```

We have grouped all the endpoint definitions inside the `PeopleHandler.MapEndpoints` static method, which takes the `IEndpointRouteBuilder` interface as an argument, which in turn is implemented by the `WebApplication` class. Then, instead of using lambda expressions, we have created separate methods for each handler, so that the code is much cleaner. In this way, to register all these handlers in our minimal API, we just need the following code in `Program.cs`:

```
var builder = WebApplication.CreateBuilder(args);
// ..
var app = builder.Build();
// ..
PeopleHandler.MapEndpoints(app);
app.Run();
```

Going forward

The approach just shown allows us to better organize a minimal API project, but still requires that we explicitly add a line to `Program.cs` for every handler we want to define. Using an interface and a bit of **reflection**, we can create a straightforward and reusable solution to simplify our work with minimal APIs.

So, let's start by defining the following interface:

```
public interface IEndpointRouteHandler
{
    public void MapEndpoints(IEndpointRouteBuilder app);
}
```

As the name implies, we need to make all our handlers (as with `PeopleHandler` previously) implement it:

```
public class PeopleHandler : IEndpointRouteHandler
{
    public void MapEndpoints(IEndpointRouteBuilder app)
    {
        // ...
    }
    // ...
}
```

> **Note**
>
> The `MapEndpoints` method isn't static anymore, because now it is the implementation of the `IEndpointRouteHandler` interface.

Now we need a new extension method that, using reflection, scans an assembly for all the classes that implement this interface and automatically calls their `MapEndpoints` methods:

```csharp
public static class IEndpointRouteBuilderExtensions
{
    public static void MapEndpoints(this
    IEndpointRouteBuilder app, Assembly assembly)
    {
        var endpointRouteHandlerInterfaceType =
          typeof(IEndpointRouteHandler);

        var endpointRouteHandlerTypes =
        assembly.GetTypes().Where(t =>
        t.IsClass && !t.IsAbstract && !t.IsGenericType
        && t.GetConstructor(Type.EmptyTypes) != null
        && endpointRouteHandlerInterfaceType
        .IsAssignableFrom(t));

        foreach (var endpointRouteHandlerType in
        endpointRouteHandlerTypes)
        {
            var instantiatedType = (IEndpointRouteHandler)
              Activator.CreateInstance
                (endpointRouteHandlerType)!;

            instantiatedType.MapEndpoints(app);
        }
    }
}
```

> **Tip**
>
> If you want to go into further detail about reflection and how it works in .NET, you can start by browsing the following page: `https://docs.microsoft.com/dotnet/csharp/programming-guide/concepts/reflection`.

With all these pieces in place, the last thing to do is to call the extension method in the `Program.cs` file, before the `Run()` method:

```
app.MapEndpoints(Assembly.GetExecutingAssembly());
app.Run();
```

In this way, when we add new handlers, we should only need to create a new class that implements the `IEndpointRouteHandler` interface. No other changes will be required in `Program.cs` to add the new endpoints to the routing engine.

Writing route handlers in external files and thinking about a way to automate endpoint registrations so that `Program.cs` won't grow for each feature addition is the right way to architect a minimal API project.

Summary

ASP.NET Core minimal APIs represent a new way of writing HTTP APIs in the .NET world. In this chapter, we covered all the pillars that we need to start developing minimal APIs, how to effectively approach them, and the best practices to take into consideration when deciding to follow this architecture.

In the next chapter, we'll focus on some advanced concepts such as documenting APIs with Swagger, defining a correct error handling system, and integrating a minimal API with a single-page application.

3
Working with Minimal APIs

In this chapter, we will try to apply some advanced development techniques available in earlier versions of .NET. We will touch on four common topics that are disjointed from each other.

We'll cover productivity topics and best practices for frontend interfacing and configuration management.

Every developer, sooner or later, will encounter the issues that we describe in this chapter. A programmer will have to write documentation for APIs, will have to make the API talk to a JavaScript frontend, will have to handle errors and try to fix them, and will have to configure the application according to parameters.

The themes we will touch on in this chapter are as follows:

- Exploring Swagger
- Supporting CORS
- Working with global API settings
- Error handling

Technical requirements

As reported in the previous chapters, it will be necessary to have the .NET 6 development framework available; you will also need to use .NET tools to run an in-memory web server.

To validate the functionality of **cross-origin resource sharing** (**CORS**), we should exploit a frontend application residing on a different HTTP address from the one where we will host the API.

To test the CORS example that we will propose within the chapter, we will take advantage of a web server in memory, which will allow us to host a simple static HTML page.

To host the web page (HTML and JavaScript), we will therefore use **LiveReloadServer**, which you can install as a .NET tool with the following command:

```
dotnet tool install -g LiveReloadServer
```

All the code samples in this chapter can be found in the GitHub repository for this book at `https://github.com/PacktPublishing/Minimal-APIs-in-ASP.NET-Core-6/tree/main/Chapter03`.

Exploring Swagger

Swagger has entered the life of .NET developers in a big way; it's been present on the project shelves for several versions of Visual Studio.

Swagger is a tool based on the OpenAPI specification and allows you to document APIs with a web application. According to the official documentation available at `https://oai.github.io/Documentation/introduction.html`:

> *"The OpenAPI Specification allows the description of a remote API accessible through HTTP or HTTP-like protocols.*
>
> *An API defines the allowed interactions between two pieces of software, just like a user interface defines the ways in which a user can interact with a program.*
>
> *An API is composed of the list of possible methods to call (requests to make), their parameters, return values and any data format they require (among other things). This is equivalent to how a user's interactions with a mobile phone app are limited to the buttons, sliders and text boxes in the app's user interface."*

Swagger in the Visual Studio scaffold

We understand then that **Swagger**, as we know it in the .NET world, is nothing but a set of specifications defined for all applications that expose web-based APIs:

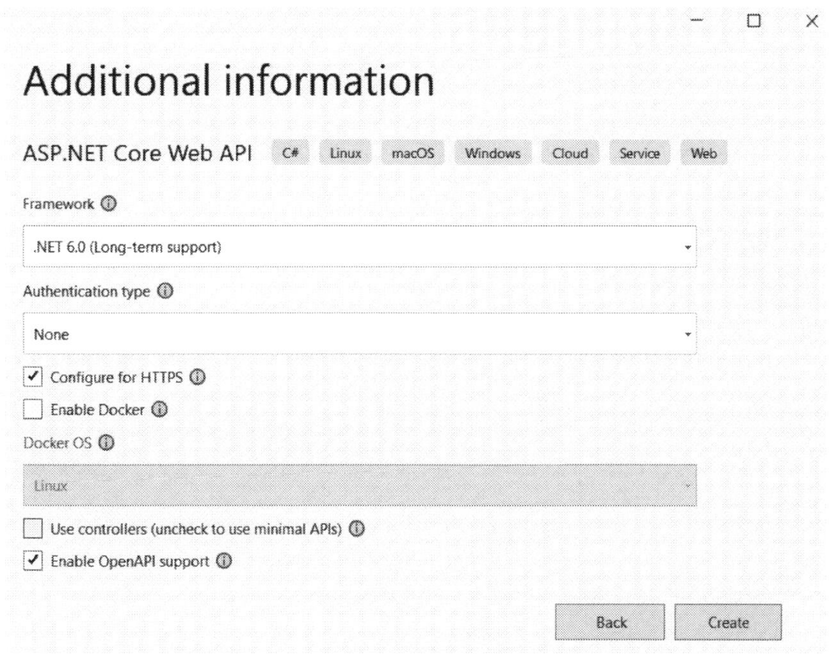

Figure 3.1 – Visual Studio scaffold

By selecting **Enable OpenAPI support**, Visual Studio goes to add a **NuGet** package called `Swashbuckle.AspNetCore` and automatically configures it in the `Program.cs` file.

We show the few lines that are added with a new project. With these few pieces of information, a web application is enabled only for the development environment, which allows the developer to test the API without generating a client or using tools external to the application:

```
var builder = WebApplication.CreateBuilder(args);
builder.Services.AddEndpointsApiExplorer();
builder.Services.AddSwaggerGen();


var app = builder.Build();


if (app.Environment.IsDevelopment())
{
    app.UseSwagger();
    app.UseSwaggerUI();
}
```

The graphical part generated by Swagger greatly increases productivity and allows the developer to share information with those who will interface with the application, be it a frontend application or a machine application.

> **Note**
> We remind you that enabling Swagger in a production environment is *strongly discouraged* because sensitive information could be publicly exposed on the web or on the network where the application resides.

We have seen how to introduce Swagger into our API applications; this functionality allows us to document our API, as well as allow users to generate a client to call our application. Let's see the options we have to quickly interface an application with APIs described with OpenAPI.

OpenAPI Generator

With Swagger, and especially with the OpenAPI standard, you can automatically generate clients to connect to the web application. Clients can be generated for many languages but also for development tools. We know how tedious and repetitive it is to write clients to access the Web API. **Open API Generator** helps us automate code generation, inspect the API documentation made by Swagger and OpenAPI, and automatically generate code to interface with the API. Simple, easy, and above all, fast.

The @openapitools/openapi-generator-cli npm package is a very well-known package wrapper for OpenAPI Generator, which you can find at https://openapi-generator.tech/.

With this tool, you can generate clients for programming languages as well as load testing tools such as **JMeter** and **K6**.

It is not necessary to install the tool on your machine, but if the URL of the application is accessible from the machine, you can use a Docker image, as described by the following command:

```
docker run --rm \
    -v ${PWD}:/local openapitools/openapi-generator-cli
generate \
    -i /local/petstore.yaml \
    -g go \
    -o /local/out/go
```

The command allows you to generate a **Go** client using the OpenAPI definition found in the petstore.yaml file that is mounted on the Docker volume.

Now, let's go into detail to understand how you can leverage Swagger in .NET 6 projects and with minimal APIs.

Swagger in minimal APIs

In ASP.NET Web API, as in the following code excerpt, we see a method documented with C# language annotations with the triple slash (///).

The documentation section is leveraged to add more information to the API description. In addition, the ProducesResponseType annotations help Swagger identify the possible codes that the client must handle as a result of the method call:

```
/// <summary>
/// Creates a Contact.
/// </summary>
/// <param name="contact"></param>
/// <returns>A newly created Contact</returns>
/// <response code="201">Returns the newly created contact</response>
/// <response code="400">If the contact is null</response>
[HttpPost]
[ProducesResponseType(StatusCodes.Status201Created)]
[ProducesResponseType(StatusCodes.Status400BadRequest)]
public async Task<IActionResult> Create(Contact contactItem)
{
    _context.Contacts.Add(contactItem);
    await _context.SaveChangesAsync();

    return CreatedAtAction(nameof(Get), new { id =
    contactItem.Id }, contactItem);
}
```

Swagger, in addition to the annotations on single methods, is also instructed by the documentation of the language to give further information to those who will then have to use the API application. A description of the methods of the parameters is always welcome by those who will have to interface; unfortunately, it is not possible to exploit this functionality in the minimal API.

Let's go in order and see how to start using Swagger on a single method:

```
var builder = WebApplication.CreateBuilder(args);
builder.Services.AddEndpointsApiExplorer();
builder.Services.AddSwaggerGen(c =>
{
```

```
    c.SwaggerDoc("v1", new()
    {
        Title = builder.Environment.ApplicationName,
        Version = "v1", Contact = new()
        { Name = "PacktAuthor", Email = "authors@packtpub.com",
          Url = new Uri("https://www.packtpub.com/") },
          Description = "PacktPub Minimal API - Swagger",
          License = new Microsoft.OpenApi.Models.
            OpenApiLicense(),
          TermsOfService = new("https://www.packtpub.com/")
});
});

var app = builder.Build();
if (app.Environment.IsDevelopment())
{
    app.UseSwagger();
    app.UseSwaggerUI();
}
```

With this first example, we have configured Swagger and general Swagger information. We have included additional information that enriches Swagger's UI. The only mandatory information is the title, while the version, contact, description, license, and terms of service are optional.

The `UseSwaggerUI()` method automatically configures where to put the UI and the JSON file describing the API with the OpenAPI format.

Here is the result at the graphical level:

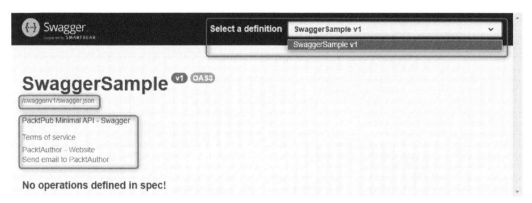

Figure 3.2 – The Swagger UI

We can immediately see that the OpenAPI contract information has been placed in the `/swagger/v1/swagger.json` path.

The contact information is populated, but no operations are reported as we haven't entered any yet. Should the API have versioning? In the top-right section, we can select the available operations for each version.

We can customize the Swagger URL and insert the documentation on a new path; the important thing is to redefine `SwaggerEndpoint`, as follows:

```
app.UseSwaggerUI(c => c.SwaggerEndpoint("/swagger/v1/swagger.
json", $"{builder.Environment.ApplicationName} v1"));
```

Let's now go on to add the endpoints that describe the business logic.

It is very important to define `RouteHandlerBuilder` because it allows us to describe all the properties of the endpoint that we have written in code.

The UI of Swagger must be enriched as much as possible; we must describe at best what the minimal APIs allow us to specify. Unfortunately, not all the functionalities are available, as in ASP.NET Web API.

Versioning in minimal APIs

Versioning in minimal APIs is not handled in the framework functionality; as a result, even Swagger cannot handle UI-side API versioning. So, we observe that when we go to the **Select a definition** section shown in *Figure 3.2*, only one entry for the current version of the API is visible.

Swagger features

We just realized that not all features are available in Swagger; let's now explore what is available instead. To describe the possible output values of an endpoint, we can call functions that can be called after the handler, such as the `Produces` or `WithTags` functions, which we are now going to explore.

The `Produces` function decorates the endpoint with all the possible responses that the client should be able to manage. We can add the name of the operation ID; this information will not appear in the Swagger screen, but it will be the name with which the client will create the method to call the endpoint. `OperationId` is the unique name of the operation made available by the handler.

To exclude an endpoint from the API description, you need to call `ExcludeFromDescription()`. This function is rarely used, but it is very useful in cases where you don't want to expose endpoints to programmers who are developing the frontend because that particular endpoint is used by a machine application.

Finally, we can add and tag the various endpoints and segment them for better client management:

```
app.MapGet("/sampleresponse", () =>
    {
        return Results.Ok(new ResponseData("My Response"));
    })
    .Produces<ResponseData>(StatusCodes.Status200OK)
    .WithTags("Sample")
    .WithName("SampleResponseOperation"); // operation ids to
                                          Open API

app.MapGet("/sampleresponseskipped", () =>
{
    return Results.Ok(new ResponseData("My Response Skipped"));
})
    .ExcludeFromDescription();

app.MapGet("/{id}", (int id) => Results.Ok(id));
app.MapPost("/", (ResponseData data) => Results.Ok(data))
    .Accepts<ResponseData>(MediaTypeNames.Application.Json);
```

This is the graphical result of Swagger; as I anticipated earlier, the tags and operation IDs are not shown by the web client:

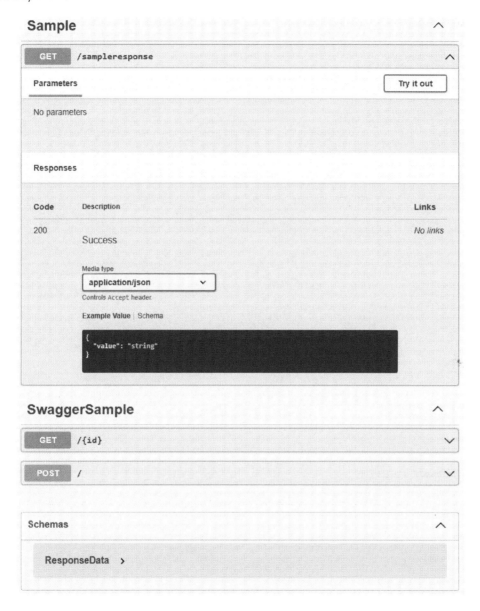

Figure 3.3 – Swagger UI methods

The endpoint description, on the other hand, is very useful to include. It's very easy to implement: just insert C# comments in the method (just insert three slashes, ///, in the method). Minimal APIs don't have methods like we are used to in web-based controllers, so they are not natively supported.

Swagger isn't just the GUI we're used to seeing. Above all, Swagger is the JSON file that supports the OpenAPI specification, of which the latest version is 3.1.0.

In the following snippet, we show the section containing the description of the first endpoint that we inserted in the API. We can infer both the tag and the operation ID; this information will be used by those who will interface with the API:

```json
"paths": {
        "/sampleresponse": {
            "get": {
                "tags": [
                    "Sample"
                ],
                "operationId": "SampleResponseOperation",
                "responses": {
                    "200": {
                            "description": "Success",
                            "content": {
                                "application/json": {
                                    "schema": {
                                        "$ref": "#/
components/schemas/ResponseData"
                                    }
                                }
                            }
                    }
                }
            }
        },
```

In this section, we have seen how to configure Swagger and what is currently not yet supported.

In the following chapters, we will also see how to configure OpenAPI, both for the OpenID Connect standard and authentication via the API key.

In the preceding code snippet of the Swagger UI, Swagger makes the schematics of the objects involved available, both inbound to the various endpoints and outbound from them.

Schemas ∧

```
ComplexResponseData ⌄ {
    value                 string
                          nullable: true
    number                integer($int32)
    money                 number($double)
    date                  string($date-time)
}


ResponseData ⌄ {
    value                 string
                          nullable: true
}
```

Figure 3.4 – Input and output data schema

We will learn how to deal with these objects and how to validate and define them in *Chapter 6, Exploring Validation and Mapping.*

Swagger OperationFilter

The operation filter allows you to add behavior to all operations shown by Swagger. In the following example, we'll show you how to add an HTTP header to a particular call, filtering it by `OperationId`.

When you go to define an operation filter, you can also set filters based on routes, tags, and operation IDs:

```
public class CorrelationIdOperationFilter : IOperationFilter
{
    private readonly IWebHostEnvironment environment;
    public CorrelationIdOperationFilter(IWebHostEnvironment
    environment)
    {
        this.environment = environment;
```

```
    }

    /// <summary>
    /// Apply header in parameter Swagger.
    /// We add default value in parameter for developer
        environment
    /// </summary>
    /// <param name="operation"></param>
    /// <param name="context"></param>
    public void Apply(OpenApiOperation operation,
    OperationFilterContext context)
    {
        if (operation.Parameters == null)
        {
            operation.Parameters = new
            List<OpenApiParameter>();
        }

        if (operation.OperationId ==
            "SampleResponseOperation")
        {
            operation.Parameters.Add(new OpenApiParameter
            {
                Name = "x-correlation-id",
                In = ParameterLocation.Header,
                Required = false,
                Schema = new OpenApiSchema { Type =
                "String", Default = new OpenApiString("42") }
            });
        }

        }
}
```

To define an operation filter, the `IOperationFilter` interface must be implemented.

In the constructor, you can define all interfaces or objects that have been previously registered in the dependency inject engine.

The filter then consists of a single method, called `Apply`, which provides two objects:

- `OpenApiOperation`: An operation where we can add parameters or check the operation ID of the current call

- `OperationFilterContext`: The filter context that allows you to read `ApiDescription`, where you can find the URL of the current endpoint

Finally, to enable the operation filter in Swagger, we will need to register it inside the `SwaggerGen` method.

In this method, we should then add the filter, as follows:

```
builder.Services.AddSwaggerGen(c =>
{
        … removed for brevity
        c.OperationFilter<CorrelationIdOperationFilter>();
});
```

Here is the result at the UI level; in the endpoint and only for a particular operation ID, we would have a new mandatory header with a default parameter that, in development, will not have to be inserted:

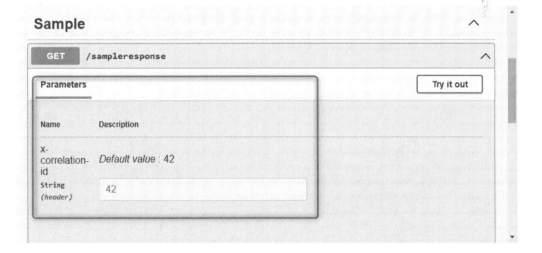

Figure 3.5 – API key section

This case study helps us a lot when we have an API key that we need to set up and we don't want to insert it on every single call.

> **Operation filter in production**
>
> Since Swagger should not be enabled in the production environment, the filter and its default value will not create application security problems.
>
> We recommend that you disable Swagger in the production environment.

In this section, we figured out how to enable a UI tool that describes the API and allows us to test it. In the next section, we will see how to enable the call between **single-page applications (SPAs)** and the backend via CORS.

Enabling CORS

CORS is a security mechanism whereby an HTTP/S request is blocked if it arrives from a different domain than the one where the application is hosted. More information can be found in the Microsoft documentation or on the Mozilla site for developers.

A browser prevents a web page from making requests to a domain other than the domain that serves that web page. A web page, SPA, or server-side web page can make HTTP requests to several backend APIs that are hosted in different origins.

This restriction is called the **same-origin policy**. The same-origin policy prevents a malicious site from reading data from another site. Browsers don't block HTTP requests but do block response data.

We, therefore, understand that the CORS qualification, as it relates to safety, must be evaluated with caution.

The most common scenario is that of SPAs that are released on web servers with different web addresses than the web server hosting the minimal API:

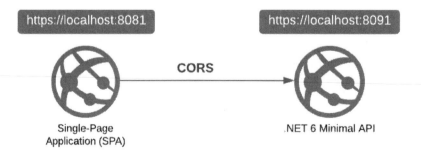

Figure 3.6 – SPA and minimal API

A similar scenario is that of microservices, which need to talk to each other. Each microservice will reside at a particular web address that will be different from the others.

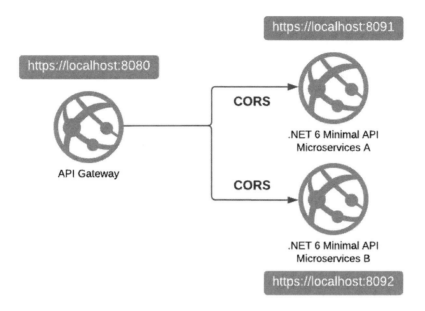

Figure 3.7 – Microservices and minimal APIs

In all these cases, therefore, a CORS problem is encountered.

We now understand the cases in which a CORS request can occur. Now let's see what the correct HTTP request flow is and how the browser handles the request.

CORS flow from an HTTP request

What happens when a call leaves the browser for a different address other than the one where the frontend is hosted?

The HTTP call is executed and it goes all the way to the backend code, which executes correctly.

The response, with the correct data inside, is blocked by the browser. That's why when we execute a call with Postman, Fiddler, or any HTTP client, the response reaches us correctly.

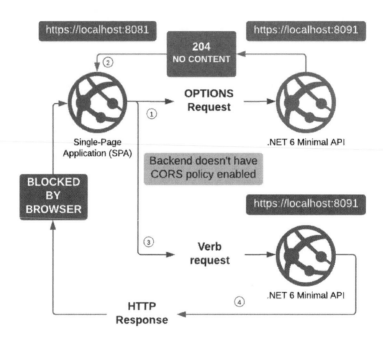

Figure 3.8 – CORS flow

In the following figure, we can see that the browser makes the first call with the OPTIONS method, to which the backend responds correctly with a 204 status code:

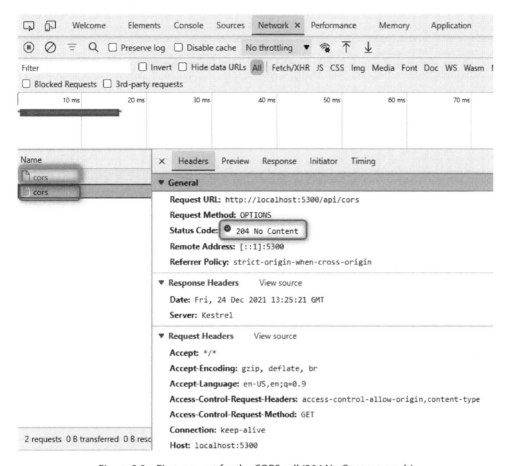

Figure 3.9 – First request for the CORS call (204 No Content result)

In the second call that the browser makes, an error occurs; the `strict-origin-when-cross-origin` value is shown in **Referrer Policy**, which indicates the refusal by the browser to accept data from the backend:

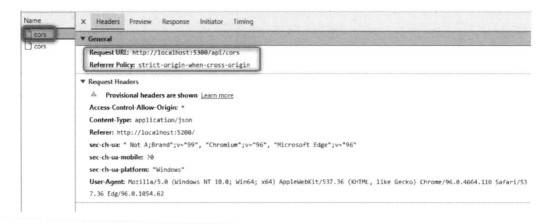

Figure 3.10 – Second request for the CORS call (blocked by the browser)

When CORS is enabled, in the response to the `OPTIONS` method call, three headers are inserted with the characteristics that the backend is willing to respect:

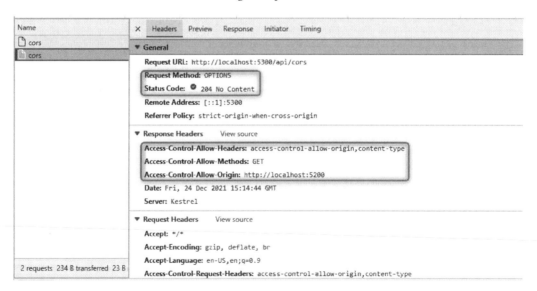

Figure 3.11 – Request for CORS call (with CORS enabled)

In this case, we can see that three headers are added that define `Access-Control-Allow-Headers`, `Access-Control-Allow-Methods`, and `Access-Control-Allow-Origin`.

The browser with this information can accept or block the response to this API.

Setting CORS with a policy

Many configurations are possible within a .NET 6 application for activating CORS. We can define authorization policies in which the four available settings can be configured. CORS can also be activated by adding extension methods or annotations.

But let us proceed in order.

The `CorsPolicyBuilder` class allows us to define what is allowed or not allowed within the CORS acceptance policy.

We have, therefore, the possibility to set different methods, for example:

- `AllowAnyHeader`
- `AllowAnyMethod`
- `AllowAnyOrigin`
- `AllowCredentials`

While the first three methods are descriptive and allow us to enable any settings relating to the header, method, and origin of the HTTP call, respectively, `AllowCredentials` allows us to include the cookie with the authentication credentials.

> **CORS policy recommendations**
> We recommend that you don't use the `AllowAny` methods but instead filter out the necessary information to allow for greater security. As a best practice, when enabling CORS, we recommend the use of these methods:

- `WithExposedHeaders`
- `WithHeaders`
- `WithOrigins`

To simulate a scenario for CORS, we created a simple frontend application with three different buttons. Each button allows you to test one of the possible configurations of CORS within the minimal API. We will explain these configurations in a few lines.

To enable the CORS scenario, we have created a single-page application that can be launched on a web server in memory. We have used `LiveReloadServer`, a tool that can be installed with the .NET CLI. We talked about it at the start of the chapter and now it's time to use it.

After installing it, you need to launch the SPA with the following command:

```
livereloadserver "{BasePath}\Chapter03\2-CorsSample\Frontend"
```

Here, `BasePath` is the folder where you are going to download the examples available on GitHub.

Then you must start the application backend, either through Visual Studio or Visual Studio Code or through the .NET CLI with the following command:

```
dotnet run .\Backend\CorsSample.csproj
```

We've figured out how to start an example that highlights the CORS problem; now we need to configure the server to accept the request and inform the browser that it is aware that the request is coming from a different source.

Next, we will talk about policy configuration. We will understand the characteristics of the default policy as well as how to create a custom one.

Configuring a default policy

To configure a single CORS enabling policy, you need to define the behavior in the `Program.cs` file and add the desired configurations. Let's implement a policy and define it as `Default`.

Then, to enable the policy for the whole application, simply add `app.UseCors();` before defining the handlers:

```
var builder = WebApplication.CreateBuilder(args);
var corsPolicy = new CorsPolicyBuilder("http://localhost:5200")
    .AllowAnyHeader()
    .AllowAnyMethod()
    .Build();
builder.Services.AddCors(c => c.AddDefaultPolicy(corsPolicy));

var app = builder.Build();
app.UseCors();
app.MapGet("/api/cors", () =>
{
```

```
            return Results.Ok(new { CorsResultJson = true });
});
app.Run();
```

Configuring custom policies

We can create several policies within an application; each policy may have its own configuration and each policy may be associated with one or more endpoints.

In the case of microservices, having several policies helps to precisely segment access from a different source.

In order to configure a new policy, it is necessary to add it and give it a name; this name will give access to the policy and allow it to be associated with the endpoint.

The customized policy, as in the previous example, is assigned to the entire application:

```
var builder = WebApplication.CreateBuilder(args);
var corsPolicy = new CorsPolicyBuilder("http://localhost:5200")
    .AllowAnyHeader()
    .AllowAnyMethod()
    .Build();

builder.Services.AddCors(options => options.
AddPolicy("MyCustomPolicy", corsPolicy));

var app = builder.Build();
app.UseCors("MyCustomPolicy");
app.MapGet("/api/cors", () =>
{
    return Results.Ok(new { CorsResultJson = true });
});
app.Run();
```

We next look at how to apply a single policy to a specific endpoint; to this end, two methods are available. The first is via an extension method to the IEndpointConventionBuilder interface. The second method is to add the EnableCors annotation followed by the name of the policy to be enabled for that method.

Setting CORS with extensions

It is necessary to use the `RequireCors` method followed by the name of the policy.

With this method, it is then possible to enable one or more policies for an endpoint:

```
app.MapGet("/api/cors/extension", () =>
{
    return Results.Ok(new { CorsResultJson = true });
})
.RequireCors("MyCustomPolicy");
```

Setting CORS with an annotation

The second method is to add the `EnableCors` annotation followed by the name of the policy to be enabled for that method:

```
app.MapGet("/api/cors/annotation",
[EnableCors("MyCustomPolicy")] () =>
{
    return Results.Ok(new { CorsResultJson = true });
});
```

Regarding controller programming, it soon becomes apparent that it is not possible to apply a policy to all methods of a particular controller. It is also not possible to group controllers and enable the policy. It is therefore necessary to apply the individual policy to the method or the entire application.

In this section, we found out how to configure browser protection for applications hosted on different domains.

In the next section, we will start configuring our applications.

Working with global API settings

We have just defined how you can load data with the `options` pattern within an ASP.NET application. In this section, we want to describe how you can configure an application and take advantage of everything we saw in the previous section.

With the birth of **.NET Core**, the standard has moved from the `Web.config` file to the `appsettings.json` file. The configurations can also be read from other sources, such as other file formats like the old `.ini` file or a positional file.

In minimal APIs, the `options` pattern feature remains unchanged, but in the next few paragraphs, we will see how to reuse the interfaces or the `appsettings.json` file structure.

Configuration in .NET 6

The object provided from .NET is `IConfiguration`, which allows us to read some specific configurations inside the `appsettings` file.

But, as described earlier, this interface does much more than just access a file for reading.

The following extract from the official documentation helps us understand how the interface is the generic access point that allows us to access the data inserted in various services:

> *Configuration in ASP.NET Core is performed using one or more configuration providers. Configuration providers read configuration data from key-value pairs using a variety of configuration sources.*

The following is a list of configuration sources:

- Settings files, such as `appsettings.json`
- Environment variables
- Azure Key Vault
- Azure App Configuration
- Command-line arguments
- Custom providers, installed or created
- Directory files
- In-memory .NET objects

(`https://docs.microsoft.com/aspnet/core/fundamentals/configuration/`)

The `IConfiguration` and `IOptions` interfaces, which we will see in the next chapter, are designed to read data from the various providers. These interfaces are not suitable for reading and editing the configuration file while the program is running.

The `IConfiguration` interface is available through the `builder` object, `builder.Configuration`, which provides all the methods needed to read a value, an object, or a connection string.

After looking at one of the most important interfaces that we will use to configure the application, we want to define good development practices and use a fundamental building block for any developer: namely, classes. Copying the configuration into a class will allow us to better enjoy the content anywhere in the code.

We define classes containing a property and classes corresponding `appsettings` file:

Configuration classes

```
public class MyCustomObject
{
    public string? CustomProperty { get; init; }
}
public class MyCustomStartupObject
{
    public string? CustomProperty { get; init; }
}
```

And here, we bring back the corresponding JSON of the C# class that we just saw:

appsettings.json definition

```
{
    "MyCustomObject": {
        "CustomProperty": "PropertyValue"
    },
    "MyCustomStartupObject": {
        "CustomProperty": "PropertyValue"
    },
    "ConnectionStrings": {
        "Default": "MyConnectionstringValueInAppsettings"
    }
}
```

Next, we will be performing several operations.

The first operation we perform creates an instance of the `startupConfig` object that will be of the `MyCustomStartupObject` type. To populate the instance of this object, through `IConfiguration`, we are going to read the data from the section called `MyCustomStartupObject`:

```
var startupConfig = builder.Configuration.
GetSection(nameof(MyCustomStartupObject)).
Get<MyCustomStartupObject>();
```

The newly created object can then be used in the various handlers of the minimal APIs.

Instead, in this second operation, we use the dependency injection engine to request the instance of the `IConfiguration` object:

```
app.MapGet("/read/configurations", (IConfiguration
configuration) =>
{
    var customObject = configuration.
    GetSection(nameof(MyCustomObject)).Get<MyCustomObject>();
```

With the `IConfiguration` object, we will retrieve the data similarly to the operation just described. We select the `GetSection(nameof(MyCustomObject))` section and type the object with the `Get<T>()` method.

Finally, in these last two examples, we read a single key, present at the root level of the `appsettings` file:

```
MyCustomValue = configuration.
GetValue<string>("MyCustomValue"),

ConnectionString = configuration.
GetConnectionString("Default"),
```

The `configuration.GetValue<T>("JsonRootKey")` method extracts the value of a key and converts it into an object; this method is used to read strings or numbers from a root-level property.

In the next line, we can see how you can leverage an `IConfiguration` method to read `ConnectionString`.

In the `appsettings` file, *connection strings* are placed in a specific section, `ConnectionStrings`, that allows you to name the string and read it. Multiple connection strings can be placed in this section to exploit it in different objects.

In the configuration provider for Azure App Service, connection strings should be entered with a prefix that also indicates the SQL provider you are trying to use, as described in the following link: `https://docs.microsoft.com/azure/app-service/configure-common#configure-connection-strings`.

At runtime, connection strings are available as environment variables, prefixed with the following connection types:

- SQLServer: `SQLCONNSTR_`
- MySQL: `MYSQLCONNSTR_`
- SQLAzure: `SQLAZURECONNSTR_`

- Custom: CUSTOMCONNSTR_

- PostgreSQL: POSTGRESQLCONNSTR_

For completeness, we will bring back the entire code just described in order to have a better general picture of how to exploit the IConfiguration object inside the code:

```
var builder = WebApplication.CreateBuilder(args);
var startupConfig = builder.Configuration.
GetSection(nameof(MyCustomStartupObject)).
Get<MyCustomStartupObject>();

app.MapGet("/read/configurations", (IConfiguration
configuration) =>
{
    var customObject = configuration.GetSection
    (nameof(MyCustomObject)).Get<MyCustomObject>();
    return Results.Ok(new
    {
        MyCustomValue = configuration.GetValue
        <string>("MyCustomValue"),
        ConnectionString = configuration.
        GetConnectionString("Default"),
        CustomObject = customObject,
        StartupObject = startupConfig
    });
})
.WithName("ReadConfigurations");
```

We've seen how to take advantage of the appsettings file with connection strings, but very often, we have many different files for each environment. Let's see how to take advantage of one file for each environment.

Priority in appsettings files

The appsettings file can be managed according to the environments in which the application is located. In this case, the practice is to place key information for that environment in the appsettings.{ENVIRONMENT}.json file.

The root file (that is, `appsettings.json`) should be used for the production environment only.

For example, if we created these examples in the two files for the "`Priority`" key, what would we get?

appsettings.json

```
"Priority": "Root"
```

appsettings.Development.json

```
"Priority":      "Dev"
```

If it is a *Development* environment, the value of the key would result in `Dev`, while in a *Production* environment, the value would result in `Root`.

What would happen if the environment was anything other than *Production* or *Development*? For example, if it were called *Stage*? In this case, having not specified any `appsettings.Stage.json` file, the read value would be that of one of the `appsettings.json` files and therefore, `Root`.

However, if we specified the `appsettings.Stage.json` file, the value would be read from the that file.

Next, let's visit the `Options` pattern. There are objects that the framework provides to load configuration information upon startup or when changes are made by the systems department. Let's go over how.

Options pattern

The `options` pattern uses classes to provide strongly typed access to groups of related settings, that is, when configuration settings are isolated by scenario into separate classes.

The `options` pattern will be implemented with different interfaces and different functionalities. Each interface (see the following subsection) has its own features that help us achieve certain goals.

But let's start in order. We define an object for each type of interface (we will do it to better represent the examples), but the same class can be used to register more options inside the configuration file. It is important to keep the structure of the file identical:

```
public class OptionBasic
{
    public string? Value { get; init; }
}


    public class OptionSnapshot
    {
```

```
        public string? Value { get; init; }
    }

    public class OptionMonitor
    {
        public string? Value { get; init; }
    }

    public class OptionCustomName
    {
        public string? Value { get; init; }
    }
```

Each option is registered in the dependency injection engine via the `Configure` method, which also requires the registration of the `T` type present in the method signature. As you can see, in the registration phase, we declared the types and the section of the file where to retrieve the information, and nothing more:

```
builder.Services.Configure<OptionBasic>(builder.Configuration.
GetSection("OptionBasic"));
builder.Services.Configure<OptionMonitor>(builder.
Configuration.GetSection("OptionMonitor"));
builder.Services.Configure<OptionSnapshot>(builder.
Configuration.GetSection("OptionSnapshot"));
builder.Services.Configure<OptionCustomName>("CustomName1",
builder.Configuration.GetSection("CustomName1"));
builder.Services.Configure<OptionCustomName>("CustomName2",
builder.Configuration.GetSection("CustomName2"));
```

We have not yet defined how the object should be read, how often, and with what type of interface.

The only thing that changes is the parameter, as seen in the last two examples of the preceding code snippet. This parameter allows you to add a name to the option type. The name is required to match the type used in the method signature. This feature is called **named options**.

Different option interfaces

Different interfaces can take advantage of the recordings you just defined. Some support named options and some do not:

- `IOptions<TOptions>`:

  - Does not support the following:

    - Reading of configuration data after the app has started

    - Named options

  - Is registered as a singleton and can be injected into any service lifetime

- `IOptionsSnapshot<TOptions>`:

  - Is useful in scenarios where options should be recomputed on every request

  - Is registered as **scoped** and therefore cannot be injected into a singleton service

  - Supports named options

- `IOptionsMonitor<TOptions>`:

  - Is used to retrieve options and manage options notifications for `TOptions` instances

  - Is registered as a singleton and can be injected into any service lifetime

  - Supports the following:

    - Change notifications

    - Named options

    - Reloadable configuration

    - Selective options invalidation (`IOptionsMonitorCache<TOptions>`)

We want to point you to the use of `IOptionsFactory<TOptions>`, which is responsible for creating new instances of options. It has a single `Create` method. The default implementation takes all registered `IConfigureOptions<TOptions>` and `IPostConfigureOptions<TOptions>` and performs all configurations first, followed by post-configuration (`https://docs.microsoft.com/aspnet/core/fundamentals/configuration/options#options-interfaces`).

The `Configure` method can also be followed by another method in the configuration pipeline. This method is called `PostConfigure` and is intended to modify the configuration each time it is configured or reread. Here is an example of how to record this behavior:

```
builder.Services.PostConfigure<MyConfigOptions>(myOptions =>
{
    myOptions.Key1 = "my_new_value_post_configuration";
});
```

Putting it all together

Having defined the theory of these numerous interfaces, it remains for us to see `IOptions` at work with a concrete example.

Let's see the use of the three interfaces just described and the use of `IOptionsFactory`, which, along with the `Create` method and with the named options function, retrieves the correct instance of the object:

```
app.MapGet("/read/options", (IOptions<OptionBasic>
optionsBasic,
        IOptionsMonitor<OptionMonitor> optionsMonitor,
        IOptionsSnapshot<OptionSnapshot> optionsSnapshot,
        IOptionsFactory<OptionCustomName> optionsFactory) =>
{

        return Results.Ok(new
        {
            Basic = optionsBasic.Value,
            Monitor = optionsMonitor.CurrentValue,
            Snapshot = optionsSnapshot.Value,
            Custom1 = optionsFactory.Create("CustomName1"),
            Custom2 = optionsFactory.Create("CustomName2")
        });
})
.WithName("ReadOptions");
```

In the previous code snippet, we want to bring attention to the use of the different interfaces available.

Each individual interface used in the previous snippet has a particular life cycle that characterizes its behavior. Finally, each interface has slight differences in the methods, as we have already described in the previous paragraphs.

IOptions and validation

Last but not least is the validation functionality of the data present in the configuration. This is very useful when the team that has to release the application still performs manual or delicate operations that need to be at least verified by the code.

Before the advent of .NET Core, very often, the application would not start because of an incorrect configuration. Now, with this feature, we can validate the data in the configuration and throw errors.

Here is an example:

Register option with validation

```
builder.Services.AddOptions<ConfigWithValidation>().
Bind(builder.Configuration.
GetSection(nameof(ConfigWithValidation)))
.ValidateDataAnnotations();
app.MapGet("/read/options", (IOptions<ConfigWithValidation>
optionsValidation) =>
{
    return Results.Ok(new
    {
        Validation = optionsValidation.Value
    });
})
.WithName("ReadOptions");
```

This is the configuration file where an error is explicitly reported:

Appsettings section for configuration validation

```
"ConfigWithValidation": {
        "Email": "andrea.tosato@hotmail.it",
        "NumericRange": 1001
    }
```

And here is the class containing the validation logic:

```
public class ConfigWithValidation
{
    [RegularExpression(@"^([\w\.\-]+)@([\w\-]+)((\.(\w)
                      {2,})+)$")]
    public string? Email { get; set; }
    [Range(0, 1000, ErrorMessage = "Value for {0} must be
                                    between {1} and {2}.")]
    public int NumericRange { get; set; }
}
```

The application then encounters errors while using the particular configuration and not at startup. This is also because, as we have seen before, `IOptions` could reload information following a change in `appsettings`:

Error validate option

```
Microsoft.Extensions.Options.OptionsValidationException:
DataAnnotation validation failed for 'ConfigWithValidation'
members: 'NumericRange' with the error: 'Value for NumericRange
must be between 0 and 1000.'.
```

> **Best practice for using validation in IOptions**
>
> This setting is not suitable for all application scenarios. Only some options can have formal validations; if we think of a connection string, it is not necessarily formally incorrect, but the connection may not be working.
>
> Be cautious about applying this feature, especially since it reports errors at runtime and not during startup and gives an Internal Server Error, which is not a best practice in scenarios that should be handled.

Everything we've seen up to this point is about configuring the `appsettings.json` file, but what if we wanted to use other sources for configuration management? We'll look at that in the next section.

Configuration sources

As we mentioned at the beginning of the section, the `IConfiguration` interface and all variants of `IOptions` work not only with the `appsettings` file but also on different sources.

Each source has its own characteristics, and the syntax for accessing objects is very similar between providers. The main problem is when we must define a complex object or an array of objects; in this case, we will see how to behave and be able to replicate the dynamic structure of a JSON file.

Let's look at two very common use cases.

Configuring an application in Azure App Service

Let's start with Azure, and in particular, the Azure Web Apps service.

On the **Configuration** page, there are two sections: **Application settings** and **Connection strings**.

In the first section, we need to insert the keys and values or JSON objects that we saw in the previous examples.

In the **Connection strings** section, you can insert the connection strings that are usually inserted in the `appsettings.json` file. In this section, in addition to the textual string, it is necessary to set the connection type, as we saw in the *Configuration in .NET 6* section.

Figure 3.12 – Azure App Service Application settings

Inserting an object

To insert an object, we must specify the parent for each key.

The format is as follows:

```
parent__key
```

Note that there are *two* underscores.

The object in the JSON file would be defined as follows:

```
"MyCustomObject": {
        "CustomProperty": "PropertyValue"

    }
```

So, we should write `MyCustomObject__CustomProperty`.

Inserting an array

Inserting an array is much more verbose.

The format is as follows:

`parent__child__ArrayIndexNumber_key`

The array in the JSON file would be defined as follows:

```
{
    "MyCustomArray": {
        "CustomPropertyArray": [
            { "CustomKey": "ValueOne" },
            { "CustomKey ": "ValueTwo" }

        ]

    }
}
```

So, to access the `ValueOne` value, we should write the following: `MyCustomArray__CustomPropertyArray__0__CustomKey`.

Configuring an application in Docker

If we are developing for containers and therefore for Docker, `appsettings` files are usually replaced in the `docker-compose` file, and very often in the `override` file, because it behaves analogously to the settings files divided by the environment.

We want to provide a brief overview of the features that are usually leveraged to configure an application hosted in Docker. Let's see in detail how to define root keys and objects, and how to set the connection string. Here is an example:

```
app.MapGet("/env-test", (IConfiguration configuration) =>
{
    var rootProperty = configuration.
    GetValue<string>("RootProperty");
    var sampleVariable = configuration.
    GetValue<string>("RootSettings:SampleVariable");
    var connectionString = configuration.
    GetConnectionString("SqlConnection");
    return Results.Ok(new
    {
        RootProperty = rootProperty,
        SampleVariable = sampleVariable,
        Connection String = connectionString
    });
})
.WithName("EnvironmentTest");
```

Minimal APIs that use configuration

The docker-compose.override.yaml file is as follows:

```
services:
    dockerenvironment:
        environment:
                - ASPNETCORE_ENVIRONMENT=Development
                - ASPNETCORE_URLS=https://+:443;http://+:80
                - RootProperty=minimalapi-root-value
                - RootSettings__SampleVariable=minimalapi-
variable-value
                - ConnectionStrings__
SqlConnection=Server=minimal.db;Database=minimal_db;User
Id=sa;Password=Taggia42!
```

There is only one application container for this example, and the service that instantiates it is called `dockerenvironment`.

In the configuration section, we can see three particularities that we are going to analyze line by line.

The snippet we want to show you has several very interesting components: a property in the configuration root, an object composed of a single property, and a connection string to a database.

In this first configuration, you are going to set a property that is the root of the configurations. In this case, it is a simple string:

```
# First configuration
- RootProperty=minimalapi-root-value
```

In this second configuration, we are going to set up an object:

```
# Second configuration
- RootSettings__SampleVariable=minimalapi-variable-value
```

The object is called `RootSettings`, while the only property it contains is called `SampleVariable`. This object can be read in different ways. We recommend using the `Ioptions` object that we have seen extensively before. In the preceding example, we show how to access a single property present in an object via code.

In this case, via code, you need to use the following notation to access the value: `RootSettings:SampleVariable`. This approach is useful if you need to read a single property, but we recommend using the `Ioptions` interfaces to access the object.

In this last example, we show you how to set the connection string called `SqlConnection`. This way, it will be easy to retrieve the information from the base methods available on `Iconfiguration`:

```
# Third configuration
- ConnectionStrings__SqlConnection=Server=minimal.
db;Database=minimal_db;User Id=sa;Password=Taggia42!
```

To read the information, it is necessary to exploit this method: `GetConnectionString("SqlConnection")`.

There are a lot of scenarios for configuring our applications; in the next section, we will also see how to handle errors.

Error handling

Error handling is one of the features that every application must provide. The representation of an error allows the client to understand the error and possibly handle the request accordingly. Very often, we have our own customized methods of handling errors.

Since what we're describing is a key functionality of the application, we think it's fair to see what the framework provides and what is more correct to use.

Traditional approach

.NET provides the same tool for minimal APIs that we can implement in traditional development: a **Developer Exception Page**. This is nothing but middleware that reports the error in plain text format. This middleware can't be removed from the ASP.NET pipeline and works exclusively in the development environment (`https://docs.microsoft.com/aspnet/core/fundamentals/error-handling`).

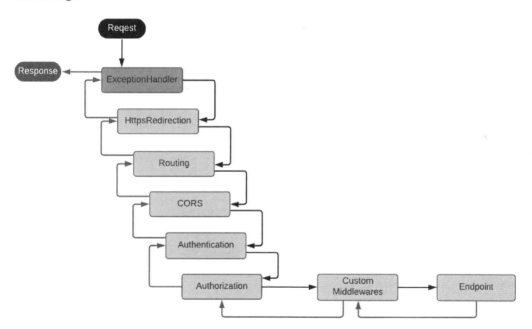

Figure 3.13 – Minimal APIs pipeline, ExceptionHandler

If exceptions are raised within our code, the only way to catch them in the application layer is through middleware that is activated before sending the response to the client.

Error handling middleware is standard and can be implemented as follows:

```
app.UseExceptionHandler(exceptionHandlerApp =>
{
    exceptionHandlerApp.Run(async context =>
    {
        context.Response.StatusCode = StatusCodes.
        Status500InternalServerError;
        context.Response.ContentType = Application.Json;
        var exceptionHandlerPathFeature = context.Features.
          Get<IExceptionHandlerPathFeature>()!;
        var errorMessage = new
        {
            Message = exceptionHandlerPathFeature.Error.Message
        };
        await context.Response.WriteAsync
        (JsonSerializer.Serialize(errorMessage));
        if (exceptionHandlerPathFeature?.
            Error is FileNotFoundException)
        {
            await context.Response.
            WriteAsync(" The file was not found.");
        }
        if (exceptionHandlerPathFeature?.Path == "/")
        {
            await context.Response.WriteAsync("Page: Home.");
        }
    });
});
```

We have shown here a possible implementation of the middleware. In order to be implemented, the UseExceptionHandler method must be exploited, allowing the writing of management code for the whole application.

Through the `var` functionality called `exceptionHandlerPathFeature = context.Features.Get<IExceptionHandlerPathFeature>()!;`, we can access the error stack and return the information of interest for the caller in the output:

```
app.MapGet("/ok-result", () =>
{
        throw new ArgumentNullException("taggia-parameter",
        "Taggia has an error");
})
.WithName("OkResult");
```

When an exception occurs in the code, as in the preceding example, the middleware steps in and handles the return message to the client.

If the exception were to occur in internal application stacks, the middleware would still intervene to provide the client with the correct error and appropriate indication.

Problem Details and the IETF standard

Problem Details for HTTP APIs is an IETF standard that was approved in 2016. This standard allows a set of information to be returned to the caller with standard fields and JSON notations that help identify the error.

HTTP status codes are sometimes not enough to convey enough information about an error to be useful. While the humans behind web browsers can be informed about the nature of the problem with an HTML response body, non-human consumers, such as machine, PC, and server, of so-called *HTTP APIs* usually cannot.

This specification defines simple JSON and XML document formats to suit this purpose. They are designed to be reused by HTTP APIs, which can identify distinct *problem types* specific to their needs.

Thus, API clients can be informed of both the high-level error class and the finer-grained details of the problem (`https://datatracker.ietf.org/doc/html/rfc7807`).

In .NET, there is a package with all the functionality that meets the IETF standard.

The package is called `Hellang.Middleware.ProblemDetails`, and you can download it at the following address: `https://www.nuget.org/packages/Hellang.Middleware.ProblemDetails/`.

Let's see now how to insert the package into the project and configure it:

```
var builder = WebApplication.CreateBuilder(args);
builder.Services.
TryAddSingleton<IActionResultExecutor<ObjectResult>,
ProblemDetailsResultExecutor>();
builder.Services.AddProblemDetails(options =>
{    options.MapToStatusCode<NotImplementedException>
     (StatusCodes.Status501NotImplemented);
});


var app = builder.Build();
app.UseProblemDetails();
```

As you can see, there are only two instructions to make this package work:

- `builder.Services.AddProblemDetails`

- `app.UseProblemDetails();`

Since, in the minimal APIs, the `IActionResultExecutor` interface is not present in the ASP.NET pipeline, it is necessary to add a custom class to handle the response in case of an error.

To do this, you need to add a class (the following) and register it in the dependency injection engine: `builder.Services.TryAddSingleton<IActionResultExecutor<ObjectResult>, ProblemDetailsResultExecutor>();`.

Here is the class to support the package, also under minimal APIs:

```
public class ProblemDetailsResultExecutor :
IActionResultExecutor<ObjectResult>
{
    public virtual Task ExecuteAsync(ActionContext context,
    ObjectResult result)
{
        ArgumentNullException.ThrowIfNull(context);
        ArgumentNullException.ThrowIfNull(result);

        var executor = Results.Json(result.Value, null,
        "application/problem+json", result.StatusCode);
```

```
        return executor.ExecuteAsync(context.HttpContext);
    }
}
```

As mentioned earlier, the standard for handling error messages has been present in the IETF standard for several years, but for the C# language, it is necessary to add the package just mentioned.

Now, let's see how this package goes about handling errors on some endpoints that we report here:

```
app.MapGet("/internal-server-error", () =>
{
    throw new ArgumentNullException("taggia-parameter",
    "Taggia has an error");
})
    .Produces<ProblemDetails>(StatusCodes.
    Status500InternalServerError)
        .WithName("internal-server-error");
```

We throw an application-level exception with this endpoint. In this case, the `ProblemDetails` middleware goes and returns a JSON error consistent with the error. We then have the handling of an unhandled exception for free:

```
{
    "type": "https://httpstatuses.com/500",
    "title": "Internal Server Error",
    "status": 500,
    "detail": "Taggia has an error (Parameter 'taggia-
    parameter')",
    "exceptionDetails": [
            {
    ------- for brevity
            }
    ],
    "traceId": "00-f6ff69d6f7ba6d2692d87687d5be75c5-
    e734f5f081d7a02a-00"
}
```

By inserting additional configurations in the `Program` file, you can map some specific exceptions to HTTP errors. Here is an example:

```
builder.Services.AddProblemDetails(options =>
{
    options.MapToStatusCode<NotImplementedException>
      (StatusCodes.Status501NotImplemented);
});
```

The code with the `NotImplementedException` exception is mapped to HTTP error code `501`:

```
app.MapGet("/not-implemented-exception", () =>
{
    throw new NotImplementedException
      ("This is an exception thrown from a Minimal API.");
})
    .Produces<ProblemDetails>(StatusCodes.
    Status501NotImplemented)
        .WithName("NotImplementedExceptions");
```

Finally, it is possible to create extensions to the `ProblemDetails` class of the framework with additional fields or to call the `base` method by adding custom text.

Here are the last two examples of `MapGet` endpoint handlers:

```
app.MapGet("/problems", () =>
{
    return Results.Problem(detail: "This will end up in
                                the 'detail' field.");
})
    .Produces<ProblemDetails>(StatusCodes.Status400BadRequest)
    .WithName("Problems");

app.MapGet("/custom-error", () =>
{
    var problem = new OutOfCreditProblemDetails
```

```
    {
        Type = "https://example.com/probs/out-of-credit",
        Title = "You do not have enough credit.",
        Detail = "Your current balance is 30,
        but that costs 50.",
        Instance = "/account/12345/msgs/abc",
        Balance = 30.0m, Accounts =
        { "/account/12345", "/account/67890" }
    };

    return Results.Problem(problem);
})
    .Produces<OutOfCreditProblemDetails>(StatusCodes.
     Status400BadRequest)
     .WithName("CreditProblems");

app.Run();

public class OutOfCreditProblemDetails : ProblemDetails
{
    public OutOfCreditProblemDetails()
    {
        Accounts = new List<string>();
    }

    public decimal Balance { get; set; }

    public ICollection<string> Accounts { get; }
}
```

Summary

In this chapter, we have seen several advanced aspects regarding the implementation of minimal APIs. We explored Swagger, which is used to document APIs and provide the developer with a convenient, working debugging environment. We saw how CORS handles the issue of applications hosted on different addresses other than the current API. Finally, we saw how to load configuration information and handle unexpected errors in the application.

We explored the nuts and bolts that will allow us to be productive in a short amount of time.

In the next chapter, we will add a fundamental building block for SOLID pattern-oriented programming, namely the dependency injection engine, which will help us to better manage the application code scattered in the various layers.

Part 2: What's New in .NET 6?

In the second part of the book, we want to show you the features of the .NET 6 framework and how they can also be used in minimal APIs.

We will cover the following chapters in this section:

- *Chapter 4, Dependency Injection in a Minimal API Project*
- *Chapter 5, Using Logging to Identify Errors*
- *Chapter 6, Exploring Validation and Mapping*
- *Chapter 7, Integration with the Data Access Layer*

4
Dependency Injection in a Minimal API Project

In this chapter of the book, we will discuss some basic topics of minimal APIs in .NET 6.0. We will learn how they differ from the controller-based Web APIs that we were used to using in the previous version of .NET. We will also try to underline the pros and the cons of this new approach of writing APIs.

In this chapter, we will be covering the following topics:

- What is dependency injection?
- Implementing dependency injection in a minimal API project

Technical requirements

To follow the explanations in this chapter, you will need to create an ASP.NET Core 6.0 Web API application. You can refer the Technical requirements section of *Chapter 2, Exploring Minimal APIs and Their Advantages* to know how to do it.

All the code samples in this chapter can be found in the GitHub repository for this book at `https://github.com/PacktPublishing/Minimal-APIs-in-ASP.NET-Core-6/tree/main/Chapter04`.

What is dependency injection?

For a while, .NET has natively supported the **dependency injection** (often referred to as **DI**) software design pattern.

Dependency injection is a way to implement in .NET the **Inversion of Control** (**IoC**) pattern between service classes and their dependencies. By the way, in .NET, many fundamental services are built with dependency injection, such as logging, configuration, and other services.

Let's look at a practical example to get a good understanding of how it works.

Generally speaking, a dependency is an object that depends on another object. In the following example, we have a `LogWriter` class with only one method inside, called `Log`:

```
public class LogWriter
{
    public void Log(string message)
    {
        Console.WriteLine($"LogWriter.Write
            (message: \"{message}\")");
    }
}
```

Other classes in the project, or in another project, can create an instance of the `LogWriter` class and use the `Log` method.

Take a look at the following example:

```
public class Worker
{
    private readonly LogWriter _logWriter = new LogWriter();

    protected async Task ExecuteAsync(CancellationToken
                                        stoppingToken)
    {
        while (!stoppingToken.IsCancellationRequested)
        {
            _logWriter.Log($"Worker running at:
            {DateTimeOffset.Now}");
            await Task.Delay(1000, stoppingToken);
        }
```

```
        }
    }
```

This class depends directly on the `LogWriter` class, and it's hardcoded in each class of your projects.

This means that you will have some issues if you want to change the `Log` method; for instance, you will have to replace the implementation in each class of your solution.

The preceding implementation has some issues if you want to implement unit tests in your solution. It's not easy to create a mock of the `LogWriter` class.

Dependency injection can solve these problems with some changes in our code:

1. Use an interface to abstract the dependency.

2. Register the dependency injection in the built-in service connecte to .NET.

3. Inject the service into the constructor of the class.

The preceding things might seem like they require big change in your code, but they are very easy to implement.

Let's see how we can achieve this goal with our previous example:

1. First, we will create an `ILogWriter` interface with the abstraction of our logger:

    ```
    public interface ILogWriter
    {
        void Log(string message);
    }
    ```

2. Next, implement this `ILogWriter` interface in a real class called `ConsoleLogWriter`:

    ```
    public class ConsoleLogWriter : ILogWriter
    {
        public void Log(string message)
        {
            Console.WriteLine($"ConsoleLogWriter.
            Write(message: \"{message}\")");
        }
    }
    ```

3.   Now, change the `Worker` class and replace the explicit `LogWriter` class with the new `ILogWriter` interface:

```
public class Worker
{
    private readonly ILogWriter _logWriter;

    public Worker(ILogWriter logWriter)
    {
        _logWriter = logWriter;
    }

    protected async Task ExecuteAsync
        (CancellationToken stoppingToken)
    {
        while (!stoppingToken.IsCancellationRequested)
        {
            _logWriter.Log($"Worker running at:
                        {DateTimeOffset.Now}");
            await Task.Delay(1000, stoppingToken);
        }
    }
}
```

As you can see, it's very easy to work in this new way, and the advantages are substantial. Here are a few advantages of dependency injection:

*   Maintainability

*   Testability

*   Reusability

Now we need to perform the last step, that is, register the dependency when the application starts up.

4. At the top of the `Program.cs` file, add this line of code:

```
builder.Services.AddScoped<ILogWriter,
ConsoleLogWriter>();
```

In the next section, we will discuss the difference between dependency injection lifetimes, another concept that you need to understand before using dependency injection in your minimal API project.

Understanding dependency injection lifetimes

In the previous section, we learned the benefits of using dependency injection in our project and how to transform our code to use it.

In one of the last paragraphs, we added our class as a service to `ServiceCollection` of .NET.

In this section, we will try to understand the difference between each dependency injection's lifetime.

The service lifetime defines how long an object will be alive after it has been created by the container.

When they are registered, dependencies require a lifetime definition. This defines the conditions when a new service instance is created.

In the following list, you can find the lifetimes defined in .NET:

- **Transient**: A new instance of the class is created every time it is requested.
- **Scoped**: A new instance of the class is created once per scope, for instance, for the same HTTP request.
- **Singleton**: A new instance of the class is created only on the first request. The next request will use the same instance of the same class.

Very often, in web applications, you only find the first two lifetimes, that is, transient and scoped.

If you have a particular use case that requires a singleton, it's not prohibited, but for best practice, it is recommended to avoid them in web applications.

In the first two cases, transient and scoped, the services are disposed of at the end of the request.

In the next section, we will see how to implement all the concepts that we have mentioned in the last two sections (the definition of dependency injection and its lifetime) in a short demo that you can use as a starting point for your next project.

Implementing dependency injection in a minimal API project

After understanding how to use dependency injection in an ASP.NET Core project, let's try to understand how to use dependency injection in our minimal API project, starting with the default project using the `WeatherForecast` endpoint.

This is the actual code of the `WeatherForecast` GET endpoint:

```
app.MapGet ("/weatherforecast", () =>
{
    var forecast = Enumerable.Range(1, 5).Select(index =>
    new WeatherForecast
    (
        DateTime.Now.AddDays(index),
        Random.Shared.Next(-20, 55),
        summaries[Random.Shared.
        Next(summaries.Length)]
    ))
    .ToArray();
    return forecast;
});
```

As we mentioned before, this code works but it's not easy to test it, especially the creation of the new values of the weather.

The best choice is to use a service to create fake values and use it with dependency injection.

Let's see how we can better implement our code:

1. First of all, in the `Program.cs` file, add a new interface called `IWeatherForecastService` and define a method that returns an array of the `WeatherForecast` entity:

    ```
    public interface IWeatherForecastService
    {
            WeatherForecast[] GetForecast();
    }
    ```

2. The next step is to create the real implementation of the class inherited from the interface.

    The code should look like this:

    ```
    public class WeatherForecastService :
    IWeatherForecastService
    {


    }
    ```

3. Now cut and paste the code from the project template inside our new implementation of the service. The final code looks like this:

    ```
    public class WeatherForecastService :
    IWeatherForecastService
    {
        public WeatherForecast[] GetForecast()
        {
            var summaries = new[]
            {
                "Freezing", "Bracing", "Chilly", "Cool",
                "Mild", "Warm", "Balmy", "Hot", "Sweltering",
                "Scorching"
            };
            var forecast = Enumerable.Range(1, 5).
            Select(index =>
            new WeatherForecast
            (
                DateTime.Now.AddDays(index),
                Random.Shared.Next(-20, 55),
                summaries[Random.Shared.Next
                (summaries.Length)]
            ))
            .ToArray();
            return forecast;
        }
    }
    ```

4. We are now ready to add our implementation of `WeatherForecastService` as a dependency injection in our project. To do that, insert the following line below the first line of code in the `Program.cs` file:

```
builder.Services.AddScoped<IWeatherForecastService,
WeatherForecastService>();
```

When the application starts, insert our service into the services collection. Our work is not finished yet.

We need to use our service in the default `MapGet` implementation of the `WeatherForecast` endpoint.

The minimal API has his own parameter binding implementation and it's very easy to use.

First of all, to implement our service with dependency injection, we need to remove all the old code from the endpoint.

The code of the endpoint, after removing the code, looks like this:

```
app.MapGet("/weatherforecast", () =>
{


});
```

We can improve our code and use the dependency injection very easily by simply replacing the old code with the new code:

```
app.MapGet("/weatherforecast", (IWeatherForecastService
weatherForecastService) =>
{
    return weatherForecastService.GetForecast();
});
```

In the minimal API project, the real implementations of the services in the service collection are passed as parameters to the functions and you can use them directly.

From time to time, you may have to use a service from the dependency injection directly in the main function during the startup phase. In this case, you must retrieve the instance of the implementation directly from the services collection, as shown in the following code snippet:

```
using (var scope = app.Services.CreateScope())
{
    var service = scope.ServiceProvider.GetRequiredService
                    <IWeatherForecastService>();
```

```
        service.GetForecast();
}
```

In this section, we have implemented dependency injection in a minimal API project, starting from the default template.

We reused the existing code but implemented it with logic that's more geared toward an architecture that's better suited to being maintained and tested in the future.

Summary

Dependency injection is a very important approach to implement in modern applications. In this chapter, we learned what dependency injection is and discussed its fundamentals. Then, we saw how to use dependency injection in a minimal API project.

In the next chapter, we will focus on another important layer of modern applications and discuss how to implement a logging strategy in a minimal API project.

5

Using Logging to Identify Errors

In this chapter, we will begin to learn about the logging tools that .NET provides us with. A logger is one of the tools that developers must use to debug an application or understand its failure in production. The log library has been built into ASP.NET with several features enabled by design. The purpose of this chapter is to delve into the things we take for granted and add more information as we go.

The themes we will touch on in this chapter are as follows:

- Exploring logging in .NET
- Leveraging the logging framework
- Storing a structured log with Serilog

Technical requirements

As reported in the previous chapters, it will be necessary to have the .NET 6 development framework.

There are no special requirements in this chapter for beginning to test the examples described.

All the code samples in this chapter can be found in the GitHub repository for this book at `https://github.com/PacktPublishing/Minimal-APIs-in-ASP.NET-Core-6/tree/main/Chapter05`.

Exploring logging in .NET

ASP.NET Core templates create a **WebApplicationBuilder** and a **WebApplication**, which provide a simplified way to configure and run web applications without a startup class.

As mentioned previously, with .NET 6, the `Startup.cs` file is eliminated in favor of the existing `Program.cs` file. All startup configurations are placed in this file, and in the case of **minimal APIs**, endpoint implementations are also placed.

What we have just described is the starting point of every .NET application and its various configurations.

Logging into an application means tracking the evidence in different points of the code to check whether it is running as expected. The purpose of logging is to track over time all the conditions that led to an unexpected result or event in the application. Logging in an application can be useful both during development and while the application is in production.

However, for logging, as many as four providers are added for tracking application information:

- **Console**: The Console provider logs output to the console. This log is unusable in production because the console of a web application is usually not visible. This kind of log is useful during development to make logging fast when you are running your app under Kestrel on your desktop machine in the app console window.

- **Debug**: The Debug provider writes log output by using the `System.Diagnostics.Debug` class. When we develop, we are used to seeing this section in the *Visual Studio* output window.

  Under the Linux operating system, information is tracked depending on the distribution in the following locations: `/var/log/message` and `/var/log/syslog`.

- **EventSource**: On Windows, this information can be viewed in the **EventTracing** window.

- **EventLog** (only when running on Windows): This information is displayed in the native Windows window, so you can only see it if you run the application on the Windows operating system.

A new feature in the latest .NET release

New logging providers have been added in the latest versions of .NET. However, these providers are not enabled within the framework.

Use these extensions to enable new logging scenarios: `AddSystemdConsole`, `AddJsonConsole`, and `AddSimpleConsole`.

You can find more details on how to configure the log and what the basic ASP.NET settings are at this link: `https://docs.microsoft.com/aspnet/core/fundamentals/host/generic-host`.

We've started to see what the framework gives us; now we need to understand how to leverage it within our applications. Before proceeding, we need to understand what a logging layer is. It is a fundamental concept that will help us break down information into different layers and enable them as needed:

Log levels	Description
Trace	Contains the most detailed messages. You can use this level when Debug is not enough. These messages are disabled by default and should *not* be enabled in production. Enabling this layer in production would put a lot of burden on the application and slow it down. Also, the amount of information written would be very complex to analyze given the large amount of data collected.
Debug	For debugging and development. These messages should *not* be enabled in production. This log level must write debugging information that is important for the developer, such as application state, data, and so on. This level must track only debug information, which is strictly necessary to verify the various states of the application.
Information	Tracks the **general flow** of the app. Messages may be stored medium to long term. Messages should be retained for future analysis or even just for history. By medium to long term, we mean that the information should be kept as long as it has meaning for the application. If the application needs to meet standards such as ISO standards, it should be retained.
Warning	Unexpected events. An unexpected event usually comprises application misbehavior, or a logic or data error that the application can incur. The application does not crash, but it does not work as expected.
Error	Indicates an error or exception in the current operation or request, not an application failure.
Critical	Shows an application failure. The message must be handled by the operator.
None	At this level, no messages will be generated.

Table 5.1 – Log levels

Table 5.1 shows the most verbose levels down to the least verbose level.

To learn more, you can read the article titled *Logging in .NET Core and ASP.NET Core*, which explains the logging process in detail here: `https://docs.microsoft.com/aspnet/core/fundamentals/logging/`.

If we select our log level as Information, everything at this level will be tracked down to the Critical level, skipping Debug and Trace.

We've seen how to take advantage of the log layers; now, let's move on to writing a single statement that will log information and can allow us to insert valuable content into the tracking system.

Configuring logging

To start using the logging component, you need to know a couple of pieces of information to start tracking data. Each logger object (`ILogger<T>`) must have an associated category. The log category allows you to segment the tracking layer with a high definition. For example, if we want to track everything that happens in a certain class or in an ASP.NET controller, without having to rewrite all our code, we need to enable the category or categories of our interest.

A category is a T class. Nothing could be simpler. You can reuse typed objects of the class where the log method is injected. For example, if we're implementing `MyService`, and we want to track everything that happens in the service with the same category, we just need to request an `ILogger<MyService>` object instance from the dependency injection engine.

Once the log categories are defined, we need to call the `ILogger<T>` object and take advantage of the object's public methods. In the previous section, we looked at the log layers. Each log layer has its own method for tracking information. For example, `LogDebug` is the method specified to track information with a `Debug` layer.

Let's now look at an example. I created a record in the `Program.cs` file:

```
internal record CategoryFiltered();
```

This record is used to define a particular category of logs that I want to track only when necessary. To do this, it is advisable to define a class or a record as an end in itself and enable the necessary trace level.

A record that is defined in the `Program.cs` file has no namespace; we must remember this when we define the `appsettings` file with all the necessary information.

If the log category is within a namespace, we must consider the full name of the class. In this case, it is `LoggingSamples.Categories.MyCategoryAlert`:

```
namespace LoggingSamples.Categories
{
    public class MyCategoryAlert
    {
    }
}
```

If we do not specify the category, as in the following example, the selected log level is the default:

```
"Logging": {
  "LogLevel": {
    "Default": "Information",
    "Microsoft.AspNetCore": "Warning",
```

```
        "CategoryFiltered": "Information",
        "LoggingSamples.Categories.MyCategoryAlert": "Debug"
    }
 }
```

Anything that comprises infrastructure logs, such as Microsoft logs, stays in special categories such as `Microsoft.AspNetCore` or `Microsoft.EntityFrameworkCore`.

The full list of Microsoft log categories can be found at the following link:

`https://docs.microsoft.com/aspnet/core/fundamentals/logging/#aspnet-core-and-ef-core-categories`

Sometimes, we need to define certain log levels depending on the tracking provider. For example, during development, we want to see all the information in the log console, but we only want to see errors in the log file.

To do this, we don't need to change the configuration code but just define its level for each provider. The following is an example that shows how everything that is tracked in the Microsoft categories is shown from the `Information` layer to the ones below it:

```
{
   "Logging": {        // Default, all providers.
     "LogLevel": {
       "Microsoft": "Warning"
     },
     "Console": { // Console provider.
       "LogLevel": {
         "Microsoft": "Information"
       }
     }
   }
}
```

Now that we've figured out how to enable logging and how to filter the various categories, all that's left is to apply this information to a minimal API.

In the following code, we inject two `ILogger` instances with different categories. This is not a common practice, but we did it to make the example more concrete and show how the logger works:

```
app.MapGet("/first-log", (ILogger<CategoryFiltered>
loggerCategory, ILogger<MyCategoryAlert> loggerAlertCategory)
=>
```

```
{
    loggerCategory.LogInformation("I'm information
      {MyName}", "My Name Information");
    loggerAlertCategory.LogInformation("I'm information
      {MyName}", "Alert Information");
    return Results.Ok();
})
.WithName("GetFirstLog");
```

In the preceding snippet, we inject two instances of the logger with different categories; each category tracks a single piece of information. The information is written according to a template that we will describe shortly. The effect of this example is that based on the level, we can show or disable the information displayed for a single category, without changing the code.

We started filtering the logo by levels and categories. Now, we want to show you how to define a template that will allow us to define a message and make it dynamic in some of its parts.

Customizing log message

The message field that is asked by the log methods is a simple string object that we can enrich and serialize through the logging frameworks in proper structures. The message is therefore essential to identify malfunctions and errors, and inserting objects in it can significantly help us to identify the problem:

```
string apples = "apples";
string pears = "pears";
string bananas = "bananas";
logger.LogInformation("My fruit box has: {pears}, {bananas},
{apples}", apples, pears, bananas);
```

The message template contains placeholders that interpolate content into the textual message.

In addition to the text, it is necessary to pass the arguments to replace the placeholders. Therefore, the order of the parameters is valid but not the name of the placeholders for the substitution.

The result then considers the positional parameters and not the placeholder names:

```
My fruit box has: apples, pears, bananas
```

Now you know how to customize log messages. Next, let us learn about infrastructure logging, which is essential while working in more complex scenarios.

Infrastructure logging

In this section, we want to tell you about a little-known and little-used theme within ASP.NET applications: the **W3C log**.

This log is a standard that is used by all web servers, not only **Internet Information Services (IIS)**. It also works on NGINX and many other web servers and can be used on Linux, too. It is also used to trace various requests. However, the log cannot understand what happened inside the call.

Thus, this feature focuses on the infrastructure, that is, how many calls are made and to which endpoint.

In this section, we will see how to enable tracking, which, by default, is stored on a file. The functionality takes a little time to find but enables more complex scenarios that must be managed with appropriate practices and tools, such as **OpenTelemetry**.

> OpenTelemetry
>
> OpenTelemetry is a collection of tools, APIs, and SDKs. We use it to instrument, generate, collect, and export telemetry data (metrics, logs, and traces) to help analyze software performance and behavior. You can learn more at the OpenTelemetry official website: `https://opentelemetry.io/`.

To configure W3C logging, you need to register the `AddW3CLogging` method and configure all available options.

To enable logging, you only need to add `UseW3CLogging`.

The writing of the log does not change; the two methods enable the scenario just described and start writing data to the W3C log standard:

```
var builder = WebApplication.CreateBuilder(args);
builder.Services.AddW3CLogging(logging =>
{
    logging.LoggingFields = W3CLoggingFields.All;
});

var app = builder.Build();
app.UseW3CLogging();

app.MapGet("/first-w3c-log", (IWebHostEnvironment
webHostEnvironment) =>
{
    return Results.Ok(new { PathToWrite =
```

```
        webHostEnvironment.ContentRootPath });
})
.WithName("GetW3CLog");
```

We report the header of the file that is created (the headers of the information will be tracked later):

```
#Version: 1.0
#Start-Date: 2022-01-03 10:34:15
#Fields: date time c-ip cs-username s-computername s-ip s-port
cs-method cs-uri-stem cs-uri-query sc-status time-taken cs-
version cs-host cs(User-Agent) cs(Cookie) cs(Referer)
```

We've seen how to track information about the infrastructure hosting our application; now, we want to increase log performance with new features in .NET 6 that help us set up standard log messages and avoid errors.

Source generators

One of the novelties of .NET 6 is the source generators; they are performance optimization tools that generate executable code at compile time. The creation of executable code at compile time, therefore, generates an increase in performance. During the execution phase of the program, all structures are comparable to code written by the programmer before compilation.

String interpolation using $" " is generally great, and it makes for much more readable code than `string.Format()`, but you should almost *never* use it when writing log messages:

```
logger.LogInformation($"I'm {person.Name}-{person.Surname}")
```

The output of this method to the Console will be the same when using string interpolation or structural logging, but there are several problems:

- You lose the *structured* logs and you won't be able to filter by the format values or archive the log message in the custom field of NoSQL products.

- Similarly, you no longer have a constant *message template* to find all identical logs.

- The serialization of the person is done ahead of time before the string is passed into `LogInformation`.

- The serialization is done even though the log filter is not enabled. To avoid processing the log, it is necessary to check whether the layer is active, which would make the code much less readable.

Let us say you decide to update the log message to include Age to clarify why the log is being written:

```
logger.LogInformation("I'm {Name}-{Surname} with {Age}",
person.Name, person.Surname);
```

In the previous code snippet, I added Age in the message template but not in the method signature. At compile time, there is no compile-time error, but when this line is executed, an exception is thrown due to the lack of a third parameter.

LoggerMessage in .NET 6 comes to our rescue, automatically generating the code to log the necessary data. The methods will require the correct number of parameters and the text will be formatted in a standard way.

To use the LoggerMessage syntax, you can take advantage of a partial class or a static class. Inside the class, it will be possible to define the method or methods with all the various log cases:

```
public partial class LogGenerator
    {
        private readonly ILogger<LogGeneratorCategory>
          _logger;

        public LogGenerator(ILogger<LogGeneratorCategory>
          logger)
        {
            _logger = logger;
        }

        [LoggerMessage(
            EventId = 100,
            EventName = "Start",
            Level = LogLevel.Debug,
            Message = "Start Endpoint: {endpointName} with
              data {dataIn}")]
        public partial void StartEndpointSignal(string
          endpointName, object dataIn);

        [LoggerMessage(
            EventId = 101,
            EventName = "StartFiltered",
            Message = "Log level filtered: {endpointName}
```

```
                 with data {dataIn}")]
        public partial void LogLevelFilteredAtRuntime(
            LogLevel, string endpointName, object dataIn);
    }


    public class LogGeneratorCategory { }
```

In the previous example, we created a partial class, injected the logger and its category, and implemented two methods. The methods are used in the following code:

```
app.MapPost("/start-log", (PostData data, LogGenerator
logGenerator) =>
{
    logGenerator.StartEndpointSignal("start-log", data);
    logGenerator.LogLevelFilteredAtRuntime(LogLevel.Trace,
        "start-log", data);
})
.WithName("StartLog");
internal record PostData(DateTime Date, string Name);
```

Notice how in the second method, we also have the possibility to define the log level at runtime.

Behind the scenes, the [LoggerMessage] source generator generates the LoggerMessage. Define() code to optimize your method call. The following output shows the generated code:

```
[global::System.CodeDom.Compiler.
GeneratedCodeAttribute("Microsoft.Extensions.Logging.
Generators", "6.0.5.2210")]
        public partial void LogLevelFilteredAtRuntime(
            global::Microsoft.Extensions.Logging.LogLevel
            logLevel, global::System.String endpointName,
            global::System.Object dataIn)
        {
            if (_logger.IsEnabled(logLevel))
            {
                _logger.Log(
                    logLevel,
                    new global::Microsoft.Extensions.
                    Logging.EventId(101, "StartFiltered"),
```

```
                    new __LogLevelFilteredAtRuntimeStruct(
                        endpointName, dataIn),
                    null,
                        __LogLevelFilteredAtRuntimeStruct.
                            Format);
            }
        }
```

In this section, you have learned about some logging providers, different log levels, how to configure them, what parts of the message template to modify, enabling logging, and the benefits of source generators. In the next section, we will focus more on logging providers.

Leveraging the logging framework

The logging framework, as mentioned at the beginning of the chapter, already has by design a series of providers that do not require adding any additional packages. Now, let us explore how to work with these providers and how to build custom ones. We will analyze only the Console log provider because it has all the sufficient elements to replicate the same reasoning on other log providers.

Console log

The `Console` log provider is the most used one because, during the development, it gives us a lot of information and collects all the application errors.

Since .NET 6, this provider has been joined by the `AddJsonConsole` provider, which, besides tracing the errors like the console, serializes them in a JSON object readable by the human eye.

In the following example, we show how to configure the `JsonConsole` provider and also add indentation when writing the JSON payload:

```
builder.Logging.AddJsonConsole(options =>
        options.JsonWriterOptions = new JsonWriterOptions()
        {
            Indented = true
        });
```

As we've seen in the previous examples, we're going to track the information with the message template:

```
app.MapGet("/first-log", (ILogger<CategoryFiltered>
loggerCategory, ILogger<MyCategoryAlert> loggerAlertCategory)
=>
{
```

```
    loggerCategory.LogInformation("I'm information
      {MyName}", "My Name Information");
    loggerCategory.LogDebug("I'm debug {MyName}",
      "My Name Debug");
    loggerCategory.LogInformation("I'm debug {Data}",
      new PayloadData("CategoryRoot", "Debug"));

    loggerAlertCategory.LogInformation("I'm information
      {MyName}", "Alert Information");
    loggerAlertCategory.LogDebug("I'm debug {MyName}",
      "Alert Debug");
    var p = new PayloadData("AlertCategory", "Debug");
    loggerAlertCategory.LogDebug("I'm debug {Data}", p);

    return Results.Ok();
})
.WithName("GetFirstLog");
```

Finally, an important note: the `Console` and `JsonConsole` providers do not serialize objects passed via the message template but only write the class name.

```
var p = new PayloadData("AlertCategory", "Debug");
loggerAlertCategory.LogDebug("I'm debug {Data}", p);
```

This is definitely a limitation of providers. Thus, we suggest using structured logging tools such as **NLog**, **log4net**, and **Serilog**, which we will talk about shortly.

We present the outputs of the previous lines with the two providers just described:

D:\Packt\Minimal-APIs-in-ASP.NET-Core-6\Chapter05\...   —   □   ×

```
{
  "EventId": 0,
  "LogLevel": "Information",
  "Category": "CategoryFiltered",
  "Message": "I\u0027m information My Name Information",
  "State": {
    "Message": "I\u0027m information My Name Information",
    "MyName": "My Name Information",
    "{OriginalFormat}": "I\u0027m information {MyName}"
  }
}
{
  "EventId": 0,
  "LogLevel": "Information",
  "Category": "CategoryFiltered",
  "Message": "I\u0027m debug PayloadData",
  "State": {
    "Message": "I\u0027m debug PayloadData",
    "Data": "PayloadData",
    "{OriginalFormat}": "I\u0027m debug {Data}"
  }
}
{
  "EventId": 0,
  "LogLevel": "Information",
  "Category": "LoggingSamples.Categories.MyCategoryAlert",
  "Message": "I\u0027m information Alert Information",
  "State": {
    "Message": "I\u0027m information Alert Information",
    "MyName": "Alert Information",
    "{OriginalFormat}": "I\u0027m information {MyName}"
  }
}
{
  "EventId": 0,
  "LogLevel": "Debug",
  "Category": "LoggingSamples.Categories.MyCategoryAlert",
  "Message": "I\u0027m debug Alert Debug",
  "State": {
    "Message": "I\u0027m debug Alert Debug",
    "MyName": "Alert Debug",
    "{OriginalFormat}": "I\u0027m debug {MyName}"
  }
}
{
  "EventId": 0,
  "LogLevel": "Debug",
  "Category": "LoggingSamples.Categories.MyCategoryAlert",
  "Message": "I\u0027m debug PayloadData",
  "State": {
    "Message": "I\u0027m debug PayloadData",
    "Data": "PayloadData",
    "{OriginalFormat}": "I\u0027m debug {Data}"
  }
}
```

Figure 5.1 – AddJsonConsole output

Figure 5.1 shows the log formatted as JSON, with several additional details compared to the traditional console log.

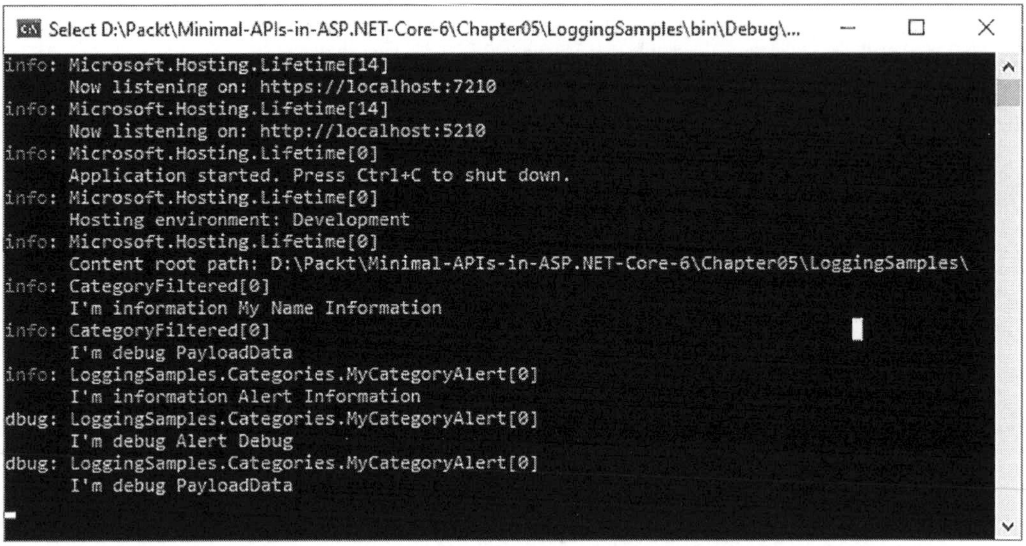

Figure 5.2 – Default logging provider Console output

Figure 5.2 shows the default logging provider Console output.

Given the default providers, we want to show you how you can create a custom one that fits the needs of your application.

Creating a custom provider

The logging framework designed by Microsoft can be customized with little effort. Thus, let us learn how to create a **custom provider**.

Why create a custom provider? Well, put simply, to not have dependencies with logging libraries and to better manage the performance of the application. Finally, it also encapsulates some custom logic of your specific scenario and makes your code more manageable and readable.

In the following example, we have simplified the usage scenario to show you the minimum components needed to create a working logging provider for profit.

One of the fundamental parts of a provider is the ability to configure its behavior. Let us create a class that can be customized at application startup or retrieve information from appsettings.

In our example, we define a fixed `EventId` to verify a daily rolling file logic and a path of where to write the file:

```csharp
public class FileLoggerConfiguration
{
        public int EventId { get; set; }
        public string PathFolderName { get; set; } =
          "logs";
        public bool IsRollingFile { get; set; }
}
```

The custom provider we are writing will be responsible for writing the log information to a text file. We achieve this by implementing the log class, which we call `FileLogger`, which implements the `ILogger` interface.

In the class logic, all we do is implement the log method and check which file to put the information in.

We put the directory verification in the next file, but it's more correct to put all the control logic in this method. We also need to make sure that the log method does not throw exceptions at the application level. The logger should never affect the stability of the application:

```csharp
public class FileLogger : ILogger
{
    private readonly string name;
    private readonly Func<FileLoggerConfiguration>
      getCurrentConfig;

    public FileLogger(string name,
      Func<FileLoggerConfiguration> getCurrentConfig)
    {
        this.name = name;
        this.getCurrentConfig = getCurrentConfig;
    }

    public IDisposable BeginScope<TState>(TState state)
      => default!;

    public bool IsEnabled(LogLevel logLevel) => true;
```

```
public void Log<TState>(LogLevel logLevel, EventId
  , TState state, Exception? exception,
  Func<TState, Exception?, string> formatter)
{
    if (!IsEnabled(logLevel))
    {
        return;
    }

    var config = getCurrentConfig();
    if (config.EventId == 0 || config.EventId ==
        eventId.Id)
    {
        string line = $"{name} - {formatter(state,
            exception)}";
        string fileName = config.IsRollingFile ?
            RollingFileName : FullFileName;
        string fullPath = Path.Combine(
            config.PathFolderName, fileName);
        File.AppendAllLines(fullPath, new[] { line });
    }
}

private static string RollingFileName =>
    $"log-{DateTime.UtcNow:yyyy-MM-dd}.txt";
private const string FullFileName = "logs.txt";
}
```

Now, we need to implement the ILoggerProvider interface, which is intended to create one or more instances of the logger class just discussed.

In this class, we check the directory we mentioned in the previous paragraph, but we also check whether the settings in the appsettings file change, via IOptionsMonitor<T>:

```
public class FileLoggerProvider : ILoggerProvider
{
    private readonly IDisposable onChangeToken;
    private FileLoggerConfiguration currentConfig;
```

```
    private readonly ConcurrentDictionary<string,
      FileLogger> _loggers = new();

    public FileLoggerProvider(
      IOptionsMonitor<FileLoggerConfiguration> config)
    {
        currentConfig = config.CurrentValue;
        CheckDirectory();
        onChangeToken = config.OnChange(updateConfig =>
        {
            currentConfig = updateConfig;
            CheckDirectory();
        });
    }

    public ILogger CreateLogger(string categoryName)
    {
        return _loggers.GetOrAdd(categoryName, name => new
          FileLogger(name, () => currentConfig));
    }

    public void Dispose()
    {
        _loggers.Clear();
        onChangeToken.Dispose();
    }

    private void CheckDirectory()
    {
        if (!Directory.Exists(currentConfig.PathFolderName))
            Directory.CreateDirectory(currentConfig.
            PathFolderName);
    }
}
```

Finally, to simplify its use and configuration during the application startup phase, we also define an extension method for registering the various classes just mentioned.

The `AddFile` method will register `ILoggerProvider` and couple it to its configuration (very simple as an example, but it encapsulates several aspects of configuring and using a custom provider):

```
public static class FileLoggerExtensions
    {
        public static ILoggingBuilder AddFile(
        this ILoggingBuilder builder)
        {
            builder.AddConfiguration();
            builder.Services.TryAddEnumerable(
              ServiceDescriptor.Singleton<ILoggerProvider,
              FileLoggerProvider>());
            LoggerProviderOptions.RegisterProviderOptions<
              FileLoggerConfiguration, FileLoggerProvider>
              (builder.Services);
            return builder;
        }

        public static ILoggingBuilder AddFile(
            this ILoggingBuilder builder,
            Action<FileLoggerConfiguration> configure)
        {
            builder.AddFile();
            builder.Services.Configure(configure);

            return builder;
        }
    }
```

We record everything seen in the `Program.cs` file with the `AddFile` extension as shown:

```
builder.Logging.AddFile(configuration =>
{
    configuration.PathFolderName = Path.Combine(
      builder.Environment.ContentRootPath, "logs");
    configuration.IsRollingFile = true;
});
```

The output is shown in *Figure 5.3*, where we can see both Microsoft log categories in the first five lines (this is the classic application startup information):

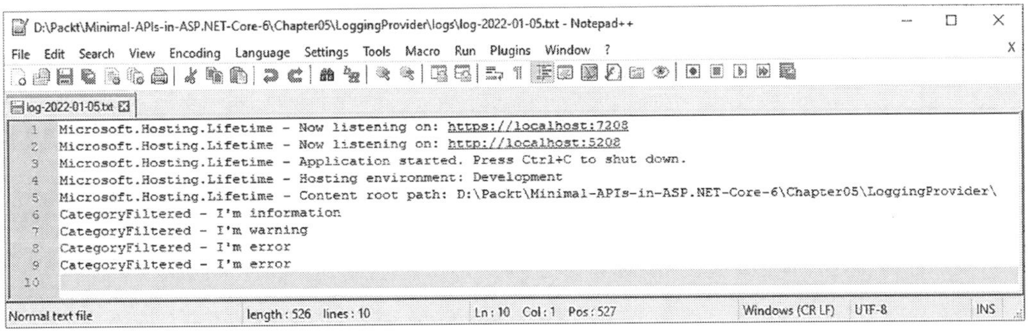

Figure 5.3 – File log provider output

Then, the handler of the minimal APIs that we reported in the previous sections is called. As you can see, no exception data or data passed to the logger is serialized.

To add this functionality as well, it is necessary to rewrite `ILogger formatter` and support serialization of the object. This will give you everything you need to have in a useful logging framework for production scenarios.

We've seen how to configure the log and how to customize the provider object to create a structured log to send to a service or storage.

In the next section, we want to describe the Azure Application Insights service, which is very useful for both logging and application monitoring.

Application Insights

In addition to the already seen providers, one of the most used ones is **Azure Application Insights**. This provider allows you to send every single log event in the Azure service. In order to insert the provider into our project, all we would have to do is install the following NuGet package:

```
<PackageReference Include="Microsoft.ApplicationInsights.
AspNetCore" Version="2.20.0" />
```

Registering the provider is very easy.

We first register the Application Insights framework, `AddApplicationInsightsTelemetry`, and then register its extension on the `AddApplicationInsights` logging framework.

In the NuGet package previously described, the one for logging the component to the logging framework is also present as a reference:

```
var builder = WebApplication.CreateBuilder(args);
builder.Services.AddApplicationInsightsTelemetry();
builder.Logging.AddApplicationInsights();
```

To register the instrumentation key, which is the key that is issued after registering the service on Azure, you will need to pass this information to the registration method. We can avoid hardcoding this information by placing it in the appsettings.json file using the following format:

```
"ApplicationInsights": {
    "InstrumentationKey": "your-key"
  },
```

This process is also described in the documentation (https://docs.microsoft.com/it-it/ azure/azure-monitor/app/asp-net-core#enable-application-insights-server-side-telemetry-no-visual-studio).

By launching the method already discussed in the previous sections, we have all the information hooked into Application Insights.

Application Insights groups the logs under a particular trace. A trace is a call to an API, so everything that happens in that call is logically grouped together. This feature takes advantage of the WebServer information and, in particular, TraceParentId issued by the W3C standard for each call.

In this way, Application Insights can bind calls between various minimal APIs, should we be in a microservice application or with multiple services collaborating with each other.

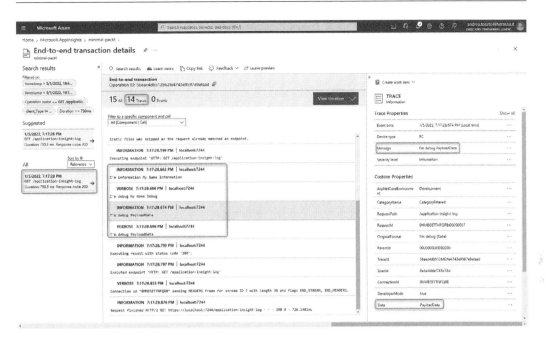

Figure 5.4 – Application Insights with a standard log provider

We notice how the default formatter of the logging framework does not serialize the `PayloadData` object but only writes the text of the object.

In the applications that we will bring into production, it will be necessary to also trace the serialization of the objects. Understanding the state of the object on time is fundamental to analyzing the errors that occurred during a particular call while running queries in the database or reading the data read from the same.

Storing a structured log with Serilog

As we just discussed, tracking structured objects in the log helps us tremendously in understanding errors.

We, therefore, suggest one of the many logging frameworks: **Serilog**.

Serilog is a comprehensive library that has many **sinks** already written that allow you to store log data and search it later.

Serilog is a logging library that allows you to track information on multiple data sources. In Serilog, these sources are called sinks, and they allow you to write structured data inside the log applying a serialization of the data passed to the logging system.

Let's see how to get started using Serilog for a minimal API application. Let's install these NuGet packages. Our goal will be to track the same information we've been using so far, specifically `Console` and `ApplicationInsights`:

```
<PackageReference Include="Microsoft.ApplicationInsights.
AspNetCore" Version="2.20.0" />

<PackageReference Include="Serilog.AspNetCore" Version="4.1.0"
/>

<PackageReference Include="Serilog.Settings.Configuration"
Version="3.3.0" />

<PackageReference Include="Serilog.Sinks.ApplicationInsights"
Version="3.1.0" />
```

The first package is the one needed for the `ApplicationInsights` SDK in the application. The second package allows us to register Serilog in the ASP.NET pipeline and to be able to exploit Serilog. The third package allows us to configure the framework in the `appsettings` file and not have to rewrite the application to change a parameter or code. Finally, we have the package to add the `ApplicationInsights` sink.

In the `appsettings` file, we create a new `Serilog` section, in which we should register the various sinks in the `Using` section. We register the log level, the sinks, the enrichers that enrich the information for each event, and the properties, such as the application name:

```
"Serilog": {
    "Using": [ "Serilog.Sinks.Console",
      "Serilog.Sinks.ApplicationInsights" ],
    "MinimumLevel": "Verbose",
    "WriteTo": [
      { "Name": "Console" },
      {
        "Name": "ApplicationInsights",
        "Args": {
          "restrictedToMinimumLevel": "Information",
          "telemetryConverter": "Serilog.Sinks.
            ApplicationInsights.Sinks.ApplicationInsights.
            TelemetryConverters.TraceTelemetryConverter,
            Serilog.Sinks.ApplicationInsights"
        }
      }
    ],
```

```
    "Enrich": [ "FromLogContext"],
    "Properties": {
      "Application": "MinimalApi.Packt"
    }
  }
}
```

Now, we just have to register `Serilog` in the ASP.NET pipeline:

```
using Microsoft.ApplicationInsights.Extensibility;
using Serilog;
var builder = WebApplication.CreateBuilder(args);
builder.Logging.AddSerilog();
builder.Services.AddApplicationInsightsTelemetry();

var app = builder.Build();
Log.Logger = new LoggerConfiguration()
.WriteTo.ApplicationInsights(app.Services.
GetRequiredService<TelemetryConfiguration>(),
TelemetryConverter.Traces)
.CreateLogger();
```

With the `builder.Logging.AddSerilog()` statement, we register Serilog with the logging framework to which all logged events will be passed with the usual `ILogger` interface. Since the framework needs to register the `TelemetryConfiguration` class to register `ApplicationInsights`, we are forced to hook the configuration to the static `Logger` object of Serilog. This is all because Serilog will turn the information from the Microsoft logging framework over to the Serilog framework and add all the necessary information.

The usage is very similar to the previous one, but this time, we add an @ (at) to the message template that will tell Serilog to serialize the sent object.

With this very simple {@Person} wording, we will be able to achieve the goal of serializing the object and sending it to the `ApplicationInsights` service:

```
app.MapGet("/serilog", (ILogger<CategoryFiltered>
loggerCategory) =>
{
    loggerCategory.LogInformation("I'm {@Person}", new
      Person("Andrea", "Tosato", new DateTime(1986, 11,
      9)));
    return Results.Ok();
```

```
})
.WithName("GetFirstLog");
internal record Person(string Name, string Surname, DateTime
Birthdate);
```

Finally, we have to find the complete data, serialized with the JSON format, in the Application Insights service.

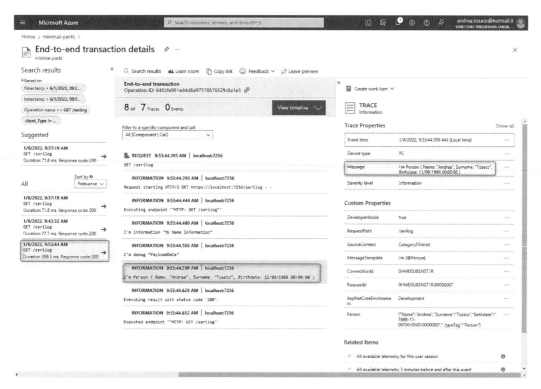

Figure 5.5 – Application Insights with structured data

Summary

In this chapter, we have seen several logging aspects of the implementation of minimal APIs.

We started to appreciate the ASP.NET churned logging framework, and we understood how to configure and customize it. We focused on how to define a message template and how to avoid errors with the source generator.

We saw how to use the new provider to serialize logs with the JSON format and create a custom provider. These elements turned out to be very important for mastering the logging tool and customizing it to your liking.

Not only was the application log mentioned but also the infrastructure log, which together with Application Insights becomes a key element to monitoring your application. Finally, we understood that there are ready-made tools, such as Serilog, that help us to have ready-to-use functionalities with a few steps thanks to some packages installed by NuGet.

In the next chapter, we will present the mechanisms for validating an input object to the API. This is a fundamental feature to return a correct error to the calls and discard inaccurate requests or those promoted by illicit activities such as spam and attacks, aimed at generating load on our servers.

6

Exploring Validation and Mapping

In this chapter of the book, we will discuss how to perform data validation and mapping with minimal APIs, showing what features we currently have, what is missing, and what the most interesting alternatives are. Learning about these concepts will help us to develop more robust and maintainable applications.

In this chapter, we will be covering the following topics:

- Handling validation
- Mapping data to and from APIs

Technical requirements

To follow the descriptions in this chapter, you will need to create an ASP.NET Core 6.0 Web API application. Refer to the *Technical requirements* section in *Chapter 2, Exploring Minimal APIs and Their Advantages*, for instructions on how to do so.

If you're using your console, shell, or bash terminal to create the API, remember to change your working directory to the current chapter number (Chapter06).

All the code samples in this chapter can be found in the GitHub repository for this book at `https://github.com/PacktPublishing/Minimal-APIs-in-ASP.NET-Core-6/tree/main/Chapter06`.

Handling validation

Data validation is one of the most important processes in any working software. In the context of a Web API, we perform the validation process to ensure that the information passed to our endpoints respects certain rules – for example, that a `Person` object has both the `FirstName` and `LastName` properties defined, an email address is valid, or an appointment date isn't in the past.

In controller-based projects, we can perform these checks, also termed **model validation**, directly on the model, using **data annotations**. In fact, the `ApiController` attribute that is placed on a controller makes model validation errors automatically trigger a `400 Bad Request` response if one or more validation rules fail. Therefore, in controller-based projects, we typically don't need to perform explicit model validation at all: if the validation fails, our endpoint will never be invoked.

> **Note**
>
> The `ApiController` attribute enables the automatic model validation behavior using the `ModelStateInvalidFilter` action filter.

Unfortunately, minimal APIs do not provide built-in support for validation. The `IModelValidator` interface and all related objects cannot be used. Thus, we don't have a `ModelState`; we can't prevent the execution of our endpoint if there is a validation error and must explicitly return a `400 Bad Request` response.

So, for example, let's see the following code:

```
app.MapPost("/people", (Person person) =>
{
    return Results.NoContent();
});

public class Person
{
    [Required]
    [MaxLength(30)]
    public string FirstName { get; set; }

    [Required]
    [MaxLength(30)]
    public string LastName { get; set; }

    [EmailAddress]
    [StringLength(100, MinimumLength = 6)]
    public string Email { get; set; }
}
```

As we can see, the endpoint will be invoked even if the `Person` argument does not respect the validation rules. There is only one exception: if we use **nullable reference types** and we don't pass a body in the request, we effectively get a `400 Bad Request` response. As mentioned in *Chapter 2, Exploring Minimal APIs and Their Advantages*, nullable reference types are enabled by default in .NET 6.0 projects.

If we want to accept a `null` body (if ever there was a need), we need to declare the parameter as `Person?`. But, as long as there is a body, the endpoint will always be invoked.

So, with minimal APIs, it is necessary to perform validation inside each route handler and return the appropriate response if some rules fail. We can either implement a validation library compatible with the existing attributes so that we can perform validation using the classic data annotations approach, as described in the next section, or use a third-party solution such as `FluentValidation`, as we will see in the *Integrating FluentValidation* section.

Performing validation with data annotations

If we want to use the common validation pattern based on data annotations, we need to rely on **reflection** to retrieve all the validation attributes in a model and invoke their `IsValid` methods, which are provided by the `ValidationAttribute` base class.

This behavior is a simplification of what ASP.NET Core actually does to handle validations. However, this is the way validation in controller-based projects works.

While we can also manually implement a solution of this kind with minimal APIs, if we decide to use data annotations for validation, we can leverage a small but interesting library, `MiniValidation`, which is available on GitHub (`https://github.com/DamianEdwards/MiniValidation`) and NuGet (`https://www.nuget.org/packages/MiniValidation`).

> **Important note**
> At the time of writing, `MiniValidation` is available on NuGet as a prerelease.

We can add this library to our project in one of the following ways:

- **Option 1**: If you're using Visual Studio 2022, right-click on the project and choose the **Manage NuGet Packages** command to open the **Package Manager GUI**; then, search for `MiniValidation`. Be sure to check the **Include prerelease** option and click **Install**.

- **Option 2**: Open the **Package Manager Console** if you're inside Visual Studio 2022, or open your console, shell, or bash terminal, go to your project directory, and execute the following command:

```
dotnet add package MiniValidation --prerelease
```

Now, we can validate a `Person` object using the following code:

```
app.MapPost("/people", (Person person) =>
{
    var isValid = MiniValidator.TryValidate(person,
      out var errors);
    if (!isValid)
    {
        return Results.ValidationProblem(errors);
    }

    return Results.NoContent();
});
```

As we can see, the `MiniValidator.TryValidate` static method provided by `MiniValidation` takes an object as input and automatically verifies all the validation rules that are defined on its properties. If the validation fails, it returns `false` and populates the `out` parameter with all the validation errors that have occurred. In this case, because it is our responsibility to return the appropriate response code, we use `Results.ValidationProblem`, which produces a `400 Bad Request` response with a `ProblemDetails` object (as described in *Chapter 3*, *Working with Minimal APIs*) and also contains the validation issues.

Now, as an example, we can invoke the endpoint using the following invalid input:

```
{
  "lastName": "MyLastName",
  "email": "email"
}
```

This is the response we will obtain:

```
{
  "type":
    "https://tools.ietf.org/html/rfc7231#section-6.5.1",
  "title": "One or more validation errors occurred.",
  "status": 400,
  "errors": {
    "FirstName": [
      "The FirstName field is required."
    ],
```

```
    "Email": [
      "The Email field is not a valid e-mail address.",
      "The field Email must be a string with a minimum
        length of 6 and a maximum length of 100."
    ]
  }
}
```

In this way, besides the fact that we need to execute validation manually, we can implement the approach of using data annotations on our models in the same way we were accustomed to in previous versions of ASP.NET Core. We can also customize error messages and define custom rules by creating classes that inherit from `ValidationAttribute`.

> **Note**
>
> The full list of validation attributes available in ASP.NET Core 6.0 is published at `https://docs.microsoft.com/dotnet/api/system.componentmodel.dataannotations`. If you're interested in creating custom attributes, you can refer to `https://docs.microsoft.com/aspnet/core/mvc/models/validation#custom-attributes`.

Although data annotations are the most used solution, we can also handle validations using a so-called fluent approach, which has the benefit of completely decoupling validation rules from the model, as we'll see in the next section.

Integrating FluentValidation

In every application, it is important to correctly organize our code. This is also true for validation. While data annotations are a working solution, we should think about alternatives that can help us write more maintainable projects. This is the purpose of `FluentValidation` – a library, part of the **.NET Foundation**, that allows us to build validation rules using a fluent interface with lambda expressions. The library is available on GitHub (`https://github.com/FluentValidation/FluentValidation`) and NuGet (`https://www.nuget.org/packages/FluentValidation`). This library can be used in any kind of project, but when working with ASP.NET Core, there is an ad-hoc NuGet package (`https://www.nuget.org/packages/FluentValidation.AspNetCore`) that contains useful methods that help to integrate it.

> **Note**
>
> .NET Foundation is an independent organization that aims to support open source software development and collaboration around the .NET platform. You can learn more at `https://dotnetfoundation.org`.

As stated before, with this library, we can decouple validation rules from the model to create a more structured application. Moreover, `FluentValidation` allows us to define even more complex rules with a fluent syntax without the need to create custom classes based on `ValidationAttribute`. The library also natively supports the localization of standard error messages.

So, let's see how we can integrate `FluentValidation` into a minimal API project. First, we need to add this library to our project in one of the following ways:

- **Option 1**: If you're using Visual Studio 2022, right-click on the project and choose the **Manage NuGet Packages** command to open **Package Manager GUI**. Then, search for `FluentValidation.DependencyInjectionExtensions` and click **Install**.

- **Option 2**: Open **Package Manager Console** if you're inside Visual Studio 2022, or open your console, shell, or bash terminal, go to your project directory, and execute the following command:

```
dotnet add package FluentValidation.
DependencyInjectionExtensions
```

Now, we can rewrite the validation rules for the `Person` object and put them in a `PersonValidator` class:

```
public class PersonValidator : AbstractValidator<Person>
{
    public PersonValidator()
    {
        RuleFor(p =>
          p.FirstName).NotEmpty().MaximumLength(30);
        RuleFor(p =>
          p.LastName).NotEmpty().MaximumLength(30);
        RuleFor(p => p.Email).EmailAddress().Length(6,
          100);
    }
}
```

`PersonValidator` inherits from `AbstractValidator<T>`, a base class provided by `FluentValidation` that contains all the methods we need to define the validation rules. For example, we *fluently* say that we have a rule for the `FirstName` property, which is that it must not be empty and it can have a maximum length of 30 characters.

The next step is to register the validator in the service provider so that we can use it in our route handlers. We can perform this task with a simple instruction:

```
var builder = WebApplication.CreateBuilder(args);
//...
builder.Services.
AddValidatorsFromAssemblyContaining<Program>();
```

The AddValidatorsFromAssemblyContaining method automatically registers all the validators derived from AbstractValidator within the assembly containing the specified type. In particular, this method registers the validators and makes them accessible through dependency injection via the IValidator<T> interface, which in turn, is implemented by the AbstractValidator<T> class. If we have multiple validators, we can register them all with this single instruction. We can also easily put our validators in external assemblies.

Now that everything is in place, remembering that with minimal APIs we don't have automatic model validation, we must update our route handler in this way:

```
app.MapPost("/people", async (Person person, IValidator<Person>
validator) =>
{
    var validationResult =
      await validator.ValidateAsync(person);
    if (!validationResult.IsValid)
    {
        var errors = validationResult.ToDictionary();
        return Results.ValidationProblem(errors);
    }

    return Results.NoContent();
});
```

We have added an IValidator<Person> argument in the route handler parameter list, so now we can invoke its ValidateAsync method to apply the validation rules against the input Person object. If the validation fails, we extract all the error messages and return them to the client with the usual Results.ValidationProblem method, as described in the previous section.

In conclusion, let's see what happens if we try to invoke the endpoint using the following input as before:

```
{
  "lastName": "MyLastName",
  "email": "email"
}
```

We'll get the following response:

```
{
  "type":
    "https://tools.ietf.org/html/rfc7231#section-6.5.1",
  "title": "One or more validation errors occurred.",
  "status": 400,
  "errors": {
    "FirstName": [
      "'First Name' non può essere vuoto."
    ],
    "Email": [
      "'Email' non è un indirizzo email valido.",
      "'Email' deve essere lungo tra i 6 e 100 caratteri.
       Hai inserito 5 caratteri."
    ]
  }
}
```

As mentioned earlier, `FluentValidation` provides translations for standard error messages, so this is the response you get when running on an Italian system. Of course, we can completely customize the messages with the typical fluent approach, using the `WithMessage` method chained to the validation methods defined in the validator. For example, see the following:

```
RuleFor(p => p.FirstName).NotEmpty().WithMessage("You must
provide the first name");
```

We'll talk about localization in further detail in *Chapter 9, Leveraging Globalization and Localization*.

This is just a quick example of how to define validation rules with `FluentValidation` and use them with minimal APIs. This library allows many more complex scenarios that are comprehensively described in the official documentation available at `https://fluentvalidation.net`.

Now that we have seen how to add validation to our route handlers, it is important to understand how we can update the documentation created by **Swagger** with this information.

Adding validation information to Swagger

Regardless of the solution that has been chosen to handle validation, it is important to update the OpenAPI definition with the indication that a handler can produce a validation problem response, calling the `ProducesValidationProblem` method after the endpoint declaration:

```
app.MapPost("/people", (Person person) =>
{
    //...
})
.Produces(StatusCodes.Status204NoContent)
.ProducesValidationProblem();
```

In this way, a new response type for the `400 Bad Request` status code will be added to Swagger, as we can see in *Figure 6.1*:

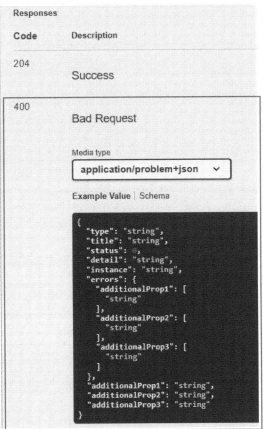

Figure 6.1 – The validation problem response added to Swagger

Moreover, the **JSON schemas** that are shown at the bottom of the Swagger UI can show the rules of the corresponding models. One of the benefits of defining validation rules using data annotations is that they are automatically reflected in these schemas:

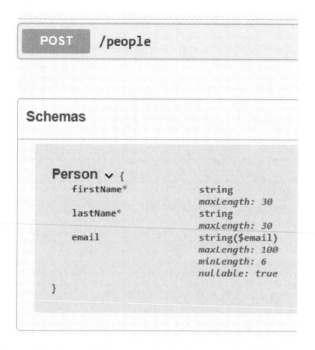

Figure 6.2 – The validation rules for the Person object in Swagger

Unfortunately, validation rules defined with `FluentValidation` aren't automatically shown in the JSON schema of Swagger. We can overcome this limitation by using `MicroElements.Swashbuckle.FluentValidation`, a small library that, as usual, is available on GitHub (`https://github.com/micro-elements/MicroElements.Swashbuckle.FluentValidation`) and NuGet (`https://www.nuget.org/packages/MicroElements.Swashbuckle.FluentValidation`). After adding it to our project, following the same steps described before for the other NuGet packages we have introduced, we just need to call the `AddFluentValidationRulesToSwagger` extension method:

```
var builder = WebApplication.CreateBuilder(args);
//...
builder.Services.AddFluentValidationRulesToSwagger();
```

In this way, the JSON schema shown in Swagger will reflect the validation rules, as with the data annotations. However, it's worth remembering that, at the time of writing, this library does not support all the validators available in `FluentValidation`. For more information, we can refer to the GitHub page of the library.

This ends our overview of validation in minimal APIs. In the next section, we'll analyze another important theme of every API: how to correctly handle the mapping of data to and from our services.

Mapping data to and from APIs

When dealing with APIs that can be called by any system, there is one golden rule: *we should never expose our internal objects to the callers*. If we don't follow this decoupling idea and, for some reason, need to change our internal data structures, we could end up breaking all the clients that interact with us. Both the internal data structures and the objects that are used to dialog with the clients must be able to evolve independently from one another.

This requirement for dialog is the reason why **mapping** is so important. We need to transform input objects of one type into output objects of a different type and vice versa. In this way, we can achieve two objectives:

- Evolve our internal data structures without introducing breaking changes with the contracts that are exposed to the callers
- Modify the format of the objects used to communicate with the clients without the need to change the way these objects are handled internally

In other words, mapping means transforming one object into another, literally, by copying and converting an object's properties from a source to a destination. However, mapping code is boring, and testing mapping code is even more boring. Nevertheless, we need to fully understand that the process is crucial and strive to adopt it in all scenarios.

So, let's consider the following object, which could represent a person saved in a database using Entity Framework Core:

```
public class PersonEntity
{
    public int Id { get; set; }

    public string FirstName { get; set; }

    public string LastName { get; set; }
```

```
    public DateTime BirthDate { get; set; }

    public string City { get; set; }
}
```

We have set endpoints for getting a list of people or retrieving a specific person.

The first thought could be to directly return `PersonEntity` to the caller. The following code is highly simplified, enough for us to understand the scenario:

```
app.MapGet("/people/{id:int}", (int id) =>
{
    // In a real application, this entity could be
    // retrieved from a database, checking if the person
    // with the given ID exists.
    var person = new PersonEntity();
    return Results.Ok(person);
})
.Produces(StatusCodes.Status200OK, typeof(PersonEntity));
```

What happens if we need to modify the schema of the database, adding, for example, the creation date of the entity? In this case, we need to change `PersonEntity` with a new property that maps the relevant date. However, the callers also get this information now, which we probably don't want to be exposed. Instead, if we use a so-called **data transformation object** (**DTO**) to expose the person, this problem will be redundant:

```
public class PersonDto
{
    public int Id { get; set; }

    public string FirstName { get; set; }

    public string LastName { get; set; }

    public DateTime BirthDate { get; set; }

    public string City { get; set; }
}
```

This means that our API should return an object of the `PersonDto` type instead of `PersonEntity`, performing a conversion between the two objects. At first sight, the exercise appears to be a useless duplication of code, as the two classes contain the same properties. However, if we consider the fact that `PersonEntity` could evolve with new properties that are necessary for the database, or change structure with a new semantic that the caller shouldn't know, the importance of mapping becomes clear. An example is storing the city in a separate table and exposing it through an `Address` property. Or suppose that, for security reasons, we don't want to expose the exact birth date anymore, only the age of the person. Using an ad-hoc DTO, we can easily change the schema and update the mapping without touching our entity, having a better separation of concerns.

Of course, mapping can be bidirectional. In our example, we need to convert `PersonEntity` to `PersonDto` before returning it to the client. However, we could also do the opposite – that is, convert the `PersonDto` type that comes from a client into `PersonEntity` to save it to a database. All the solutions we're talking about are valid for both scenarios.

We can either perform mapping manually or adopt a third-party library that provides us with this feature. In the following sections, we'll analyze both approaches, understanding the pros and cons of the available solutions.

Performing manual mapping

In the previous section, we said that mapping essentially means copying the properties of a source object into the properties of a destination and applying some sort of conversion. The easiest and most effective way to perform this task is to do it manually.

With this approach, we need to take care of all the mapping code by ourselves. From this point of view, there is nothing much more to say; we need a method that takes an object as input and transforms it into another as output, remembering to apply mapping recursively if a class contains a complex property that must be mapped in turn. The only suggestion is to use an extension method so that we can easily call it everywhere we need.

A full example of this mapping process is available in the GitHub repository: `https://github.com/PacktPublishing/Minimal-APIs-in-ASP.NET-Core-6/tree/main/Chapter06`.

This solution guarantees the best performance because we explicitly write all mapping instructions without relying on an automatic system (such as reflection). However, the manual method has a drawback: every time we add a property in the entity that must be mapped to a DTO, we need to change the mapping code. On the other hand, some approaches can simplify mapping, but at the cost of performance overhead. In the next section, we look at one such approach using `AutoMapper`.

Mapping with AutoMapper

`AutoMapper` is probably one the most famous mapping framework for .NET. It uses a fluent configuration API that works with a convention-based matching algorithm to match source values to destination values. As with `FluentValidation`, the framework is part of the .NET Foundation and is available either on GitHub (`https://github.com/AutoMapper/AutoMapper`) or NuGet (`https://www.nuget.org/packages/AutoMapper`). Again, in this case, we have a specific NuGet package, `https://www.nuget.org/packages/AutoMapper.Extensions.Microsoft.DependencyInjection`, that simplifies its integration into ASP.NET Core projects.

Let's take a quick look at how to integrate `AutoMapper` in a minimal API project, showing its main features. The full documentation of the library is available at `https://docs.automapper.org`.

As usual, the first thing to do is to add the library to our project, following the same instructions we used in the previous sections. Then, we need to configure `AutoMapper`, telling it how to perform mapping. There are several ways to perform this task, but the recommended approach is to create classes that are inherited from the `Profile` base class provided by the library and put the configuration into the constructor:

```
public class PersonProfile : Profile
{
    public PersonProfile()
    {
        CreateMap<PersonEntity, PersonDto>();
    }
}
```

That's all we need to start: a single instruction to indicate that we want to map `PersonEntity` to `PersonDto`, without any other details. We have said that `AutoMapper` is convention-based. This means that, by default, it maps properties with the same name from the source to the destination, while also performing automatic conversions into compatible types, if necessary. For example, an `int` property on the source can be automatically mapped to a `double` property with the same name on the destination. In other words, if source and destination objects have the same property, there is no need for any explicit mapping instruction. However, in our case, we need to perform some transformations, so we can add them fluently after `CreateMap`:

```
public class PersonProfile : Profile
{
    public PersonProfile()
    {
        CreateMap<PersonEntity, PersonDto>()
            .ForMember(dst => dst.Age, opt =>
```

```
        opt.MapFrom(src => CalculateAge(src.BirthDate)))
        .ForMember(dst => dst.City, opt =>
          opt.MapFrom(src => src.Address.City));
    }


    private static int CalculateAge(DateTime dateOfBirth)
    {
        var today = DateTime.Today;
        var age = today.Year - dateOfBirth.Year;
        if (today.DayOfYear < dateOfBirth.DayOfYear)
        {
            age--;
        }


        return age;
    }
}
```

With the `ForMember` method, we can specify how to map destination properties, `dst.Age` and `dst.City`, using conversion expressions. We still don't need to explicitly map the `Id`, `FirstName`, or `LastName` properties because they exist with these names at both the source and destination.

Now that we have defined the mapping profile, we need to register it at startup so that ASP.NET Core can use it. As with `FluentValidation`, we can invoke an extension method on `IServiceCollection`:

```
builder.Services.AddAutoMapper(typeof(Program).Assembly);
```

With this line of code, we automatically register all the profiles that are contained in the specified assembly. If we add more profiles to our project, such as a separate `Profile` class for every entity to map, we don't need to change the registration instructions.

In this way, we can now use the `IMapper` interface through dependency injection:

```
app.MapGet("/people/{id:int}", (int id, IMapper mapper) =>
{
    var personEntity = new PersonEntity();
    //...


    var personDto = mapper.Map<PersonDto>(personEntity);
    return Results.Ok(personDto);
```

```
})
.Produces(StatusCodes.Status200OK, typeof(PersonDto));
```

After retrieving `PersonEntity`, for example, from a database using Entity Framework Core, we call the `Map` method on the `IMapper` interface, specifying the type of the resulting object and the input class. With this line of code, `AutoMapper` will use the corresponding profile to convert `PersonEntity` into a `PersonDto` instance.

With this solution in place, mapping is now much easier to maintain because, as long as we add properties with the same name on the source and destination, we don't need to change the profile at all. Moreover, `AutoMapper` supports list mapping and recursive mapping too. So, if we have an entity that must be mapped, such as a property of the `AddressEntity` type on the `PersonEntity` class, and the corresponding profile is available, the conversion is again performed automatically.

The drawback of this approach is a performance overhead. `AutoMapper` works by dynamically executing mapping code at runtime, so it uses reflection under the hood. Profiles are created the first time they are used and then they are cached to speed up subsequent mappings. However, profiles are always applied dynamically, so there is a cost for the operation that is dependent on the complexity of the mapping code itself. We have only seen a basic example of `AutoMapper`. The library is very powerful and can manage quite complex mappings. However, we need to be careful not to abuse it – otherwise, we can negatively impact the performance of our application.

Summary

Validation and mapping are two important features that we need to take into account when developing APIs to build more robust and maintainable applications. Minimal APIs do not provide any built-in way to perform these tasks, so it is important to know how we can add support for this kind of feature. We have seen that we can perform validations with data annotations or using `FluentValidation` and how to add validation information to Swagger. We have also talked about the significance of data mapping and shown how to either leverage manual mapping or the `AutoMapper` library, describing the pros and cons of each approach.

In the next chapter, we will talk about how to integrate minimal APIs with a **data access layer**, showing, for example, how to access a database using Entity Framework Core.

7

Integration with the Data Access Layer

In this chapter, we will learn about some basic ways to add a data access layer to the minimal APIs in .NET 6.0. We will see how we can use some topics covered previously in the book to access data with **Entity Framework** (**EF**) and then with Dapper. These are two ways to access a database.

In this chapter, we will be covering the following topics:

- Using Entity Framework
- Using Dapper

By the end of this chapter, you will be able to use EF from scratch in a minimal API project, and use Dapper for the same goal. You will also be able to tell when one approach is better than the other in a project.

Technical requirements

To follow along with this chapter, you will need to create an ASP.NET Core 6.0 Web API application. You can use either of the following options:

- Click on the **New Project** option in the **File** menu of Visual Studio 2022, then choose the **ASP.NET Core Web API** template, select a name and the working directory in the wizard, and be sure to uncheck the **Use controllers** option in the next step.

- Open your console, shell, or Bash terminal, and change to your working directory. Use the following command to create a new Web API application:

```
dotnet new webapi -minimal -o Chapter07
```

Now, open the project in Visual Studio by double-clicking on the project file or, in Visual Studio Code, type the following command in the already open console:

```
cd Chapter07
code.
```

Finally, you can safely remove all the code related to the WeatherForecast sample, as we don't need it for this chapter.

All the code samples in this chapter can be found in the GitHub repository for this book at https://github.com/PacktPublishing/Minimal-APIs-in-ASP.NET-Core-6/tree/main/Chapter07.

Using Entity Framework

We can absolutely say that if we are building an API, it is very likely that we will interact with data.

In addition, this data most probably needs to be persisted after the application restarts or after other events, such as a new deployment of the application. There are many options for persisting data in .NET applications, but EF is the most user-friendly and common solution for a lot of scenarios.

Entity Framework Core (**EF Core**) is an extensible, open source, and cross-platform data access library for .NET applications. It enables developers to work with the database by using .NET objects directly and removes, in most cases, the need to know how to write the data access code directly in the database.

On top of this, EF Core supports a lot of databases, including SQLite, MySQL, Oracle, Microsoft SQL Server, and PostgreSQL.

In addition, it supports an in-memory database that helps to write tests for our applications or to make the development cycle easier because you don't need a real database up and running.

In the next section, we will see how to set up a project for using EF and its main features.

Setting up the project

From the project root, create an Icecream.cs class and give it the following content:

```
namespace Chapter07.Models;
public class Icecream
{
    public int Id { get; set; }
    public string? Name { get; set; }
```

```
        public string? Description { get; set; }
}
```

The `Icecream` class is an object that represents an ice cream in our project. This class should be called a data model, and we will use this object in the next sections of this chapter to map it to a database table.

Now it's time to add the EF Core NuGet reference to the project.

In order to do that, you can use one of the following methods:

- In a new terminal window, enter the following code to add the EF Core `InMemory` package:

  ```
  dotnet add package Microsoft.EntityFrameworkCore.InMemory
  ```

- If you would like to use Visual Studio 2022 to add the reference, right-click on **Dependencies** and then select **Manage NuGet Packages**. Search for `Microsoft.EntityFrameworkCore.InMemory` and install the package.

In the next section, we will be adding EF Core to our project.

Adding EF Core to the project

In order to store the ice cream objects in the database, we need to set up EF Core in our project.

To set up an in-memory database, add the following code to the bottom of the `Program.cs` file:

```
class IcecreamDb : DbContext
{
    public IcecreamDb(DbContextOptions options) :
      base(options) { }
    public DbSet<Icecream> Icecreams { get; set; } = null!;
}
```

`DbContext` object represents a connection to the database, and it's used to save and query instances of entities in the database.

The `DbSet` represents the instances of the entities, and they will be converted into a real table in the database.

In this case, we will have just one table in the database, called `Icecreams`.

In `Program.cs`, after the builder initialization, add the following code:

```
builder.Services.AddDbContext<IcecreamDb>(options => options.
UseInMemoryDatabase("icecreams"));
```

Now we are ready to add some API endpoints to start interacting with the database.

Adding endpoints to the project

Let's add the code to create a new item in the `icecreams` list. In `Program.cs`, add the following code before the `app.Run()` line of code:

```
app.MapPost("/icecreams", async (IcecreamDb db, Icecream
icecream) =>
{
    await db.Icecreams.AddAsync(icecream);
    await db.SaveChangesAsync();
    return Results.Created($"/icecreams/{icecream.Id}",
                           icecream);
});
```

The first parameter of the `MapPost` function is the DbContext. By default, the minimal API architecture uses dependency injection to share the instances of the DbContext.

> **Dependency injection**
>
> If you want to know more about dependency injection, go to *Chapter 4, Dependency Injection in a Minimal API Project*.

In order to save an item into the database, we use the `AddSync` method directly from the entity that represents the object.

To persist the new item in the database, we need to call the `SaveChangesAsync()` method, which is responsible for saving all the changes that happen to the database before the last call to `SaveChangesAsync()`.

In a very similar way, we can add the endpoint to retrieve all the items in the `icecreams` database.

After the code to add an ice cream, we can add the following code:

```
app.MapGet("/icecreams", async (IcecreamDb db) => await
db.Icecreams.ToListAsync());
```

Also, in this case, the DbContext is available as a parameter and we can retrieve all the items in the database directly from the entities in the DbContext.

With the `ToListAsync()` method, the application loads all the entities in the database and sends them back as the endpoint result.

Make sure you have saved all your changes in the project and run the app.

A new browser window will open, and you can navigate to the /swagger URL:

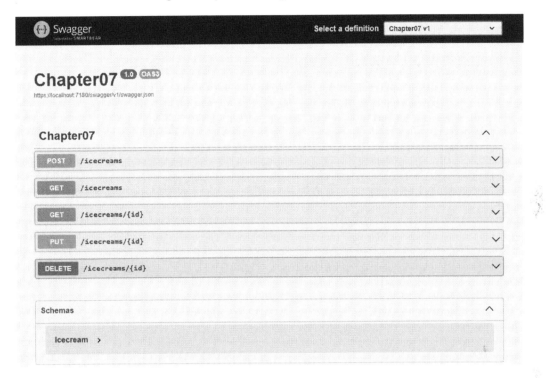

Figure 7.1 – Swagger browser window

Select the **POST/icecreams** button, followed by **Try it out**.

Replace the request body content with the following JSON:

```
{
  "id": 0,
  "name": "icecream 1",
  "description": "description 1"
}
```

Click on **Execute**:

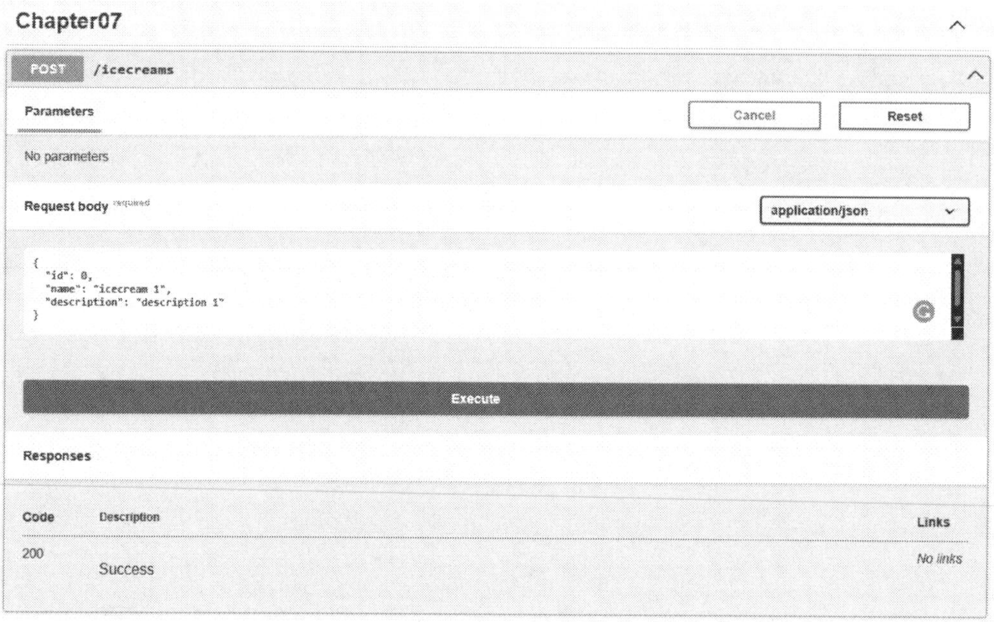

Figure 7.2 – Swagger response

Now we have at least one item in the database, and we can try the other endpoint to retrieve all the items in the database.

Scroll down the page a little bit and select **GET/icecreams**, followed by **Try it out** and then **Execute**.

You will see the list with one item under **Response Body**.

Let's see how to finalize this first demo by adding the other CRUD operations to our endpoints:

1. To get an item by ID, add the following code under the app.MapGet route you created earlier:

    ```
    app.MapGet("/icecreams/{id}", async (IcecreamDb db, int
    id) => await db.Icecreams.FindAsync(id));
    ```

    To check this out, you can launch the application again and use the Swagger UI as before.

2. Next, add an item in the database by performing a post call (as in the previous section).

3. Click **GET/icecreams/{id}** followed by **Try it out**.

4. Insert the value 1 in the id parameter field and then click on **Execute**.

5. You will see the item in the **Response Body** section.

6. The following is an example of a response from the API:

```
{
    "id": 1,
    "name": "icecream 1",
    "description": "description 1"
}
```

This is what the response looks like:

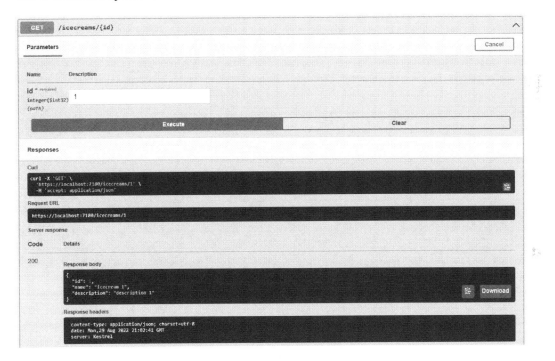

Figure 7.3 – Response result

To update an item by ID, we can create a new `MapPut` endpoint with two parameters: the item with the entity values and the ID of the old entity in the database that we want to update.

The code should be like the following snippet:

```
app.MapPut("/icecreams/{id}", async (IcecreamDb db, Icecream
updateicecream, int id) =>
{
    var icecream = await db.Icecreams.FindAsync(id);
```

```
        if (icecream is null) return Results.NotFound();
        icecream.Name = updateicecream.Name;
        icecream.Description = updateicecream.Description;
        await db.SaveChangesAsync();
        return Results.NoContent();
});
```

Just to be clear, first of all, we need to find the item in the database with the ID from the parameters. If we don't find an item in the database, it's a good practice to return a Not Found HTTP status to the caller.

If we find the entity in the database, we update the entity with the new values and we save all the changes in the database before sending back the HTTP status No Content.

The last CRUD operation we need to perform is to delete an item from the database.

This operation is very similar to the update operation because, first of all, we need to find the item in the database and then we can try to perform the delete operation.

The following code snippet shows how to implement a delete operation with the right HTTP verb of the minimal API:

```
app.MapDelete("/icecreams/{id}", async (IcecreamDb db, int id)
=>
{
    var icecream = await db.Icecreams.FindAsync(id);
    if (icecream is null)
    {
        return Results.NotFound();
    }
    db.Icecreams.Remove(icecream);
    await db.SaveChangesAsync();
    return Results.Ok();
});
```

In this section, we have learned how to use EF in a minimal API project.

We saw how to add the NuGet packages to start working with EF, and how to implement the entire set of CRUD operations in a minimal API .NET 6 project.

In the next section, we will see how to implement the same project with the same logic but using Dapper as the primary library to access data.

Using Dapper

Dapper is an **Object-Relational Mapper (ORM)** or, to be more precise, a micro ORM. With Dapper, we can write SQL statements directly in .NET projects like we can do in SQL Server (or another database). One of the best advantages of using Dapper in a project is the performance, because it doesn't translate queries from .NET objects and doesn't add any layers between the application and the library to access the database. It extends the IDbConnection object and provides a lot of methods to query the database. This means we have to write queries that are compatible with the database provider.

It supports synchronous and asynchronous method executions. This is a list of the methods that Dapper adds to the IDbConnection interface:

- Execute
- Query
- QueryFirst
- QueryFirstOrDefault
- QuerySingle
- QuerySingleOrDefault
- QueryMultiple

As we mentioned, it provides an async version for all these methods. You can find the right methods by adding the Async keyword at the end of the method name.

In the next section, we will see how to set up a project for using Dapper with a SQL Server LocalDB.

Setting up the project

The first thing we are going to do is to create a new database. You can use your SQL Server LocalDB instance installed with Visual Studio by default or another SQL Server instance in your environment.

You can execute the following script in your database to create one table and populate it with data:

```
CREATE TABLE [dbo].[Icecreams] (
    [Id] [int] IDENTITY(1,1) NOT NULL,
    [Name] [nvarchar](50) NOT NULL,
    [Description] [nvarchar](255) NOT NULL)
GO

INSERT [dbo].[Icecreams] ([Name], [Description]) VALUES
('Icecream 1','Description 1')
```

```
INSERT [dbo].[Icecreams] ([Name], [Description]) VALUES
('Icecream 2','Description 2')
INSERT [dbo].[Icecreams] ([Name], [Description]) VALUES
('Icecream 3','Description 3')
```

Once we have the database, we can install these NuGet packages with the following command in the Visual Studio terminal:

```
Install-Package Dapper
Install-Package Microsoft.Data.SqlClient
```

Now we can continue to add the code to interact with the database. In this example, we are going to use a repository pattern.

Creating a repository pattern

In this section, we are going to create a simple repository pattern, but we will try to make it as simple as possible so we can understand the main features of Dapper:

1. In the `Program.cs` file, add a simple class that represents our entity in the database:

    ```
    public class Icecream
    {
        public int Id { get; set; }
        public string? Name { get; set; }
        public string? Description { get; set; }
    }
    ```

2. After this, modify the `appsettings.json` file by adding the connection string at the end of the file:

    ```
    "ConnectionStrings": {
        "SqlConnection":
          "Data Source=(localdb)\\MSSQLLocalDB;
          Initial Catalog=Chapter07;
          Integrated Security=True;
          Connect Timeout=30;
          Encrypt=False;
          TrustServerCertificate=False;"
    }
    ```

If you are using LocalDB, the connection string should be the right one for your environment as well.

3. Create a new class in the root of the project called `DapperContext` and give it the following code:

```
public class DapperContext
{
    private readonly IConfiguration _configuration;
    private readonly string _connectionString;
    public DapperContext(IConfiguration configuration)
    {
        _configuration = configuration;
        _connectionString = _configuration
           .GetConnectionString("SqlConnection");
    }
    public IDbConnection CreateConnection()
        => new SqlConnection(_connectionString);
}
```

We injected with dependency injection the `IConfiguration` interface to retrieve the connection string from the settings file.

4. Now we are going to create the interface and the implementation of our repository. In order to do that, add the following code to the `Program.cs` file.

```
public interface IIcecreamsRepository
{
}

public class IcecreamsRepository : IIcecreamsRepository
{
    private readonly DapperContext _context;
    public IcecreamsRepository(DapperContext context)
    {
        _context = context;
    }
}
```

In the next sections, we will be adding some code to the interface and to the implementation of the repository.

Finally, we can register the context, the interface, and its implementation as a service.

5. Let's put the following code after the builder initialization in the `Program.cs` file:

```
builder.Services.AddSingleton<DapperContext>();
builder.Services.AddScoped<IIcecreamsRepository,
IcecreamsRepository>();
```

Now we are ready to implement the first query.

Using Dapper to query the database

First of all, let's modify the `IIcecreamsRepository` interface by adding a new method:

```
public Task<IEnumerable<Icecream>> GetIcecreams();
```

Then, let's implement this method in the `IcecreamsRepository` class:

```
public async Task<IEnumerable<Icecream>> GetIcecreams()
{
    var query = "SELECT * FROM Icecreams";
    using (var connection = _context.CreateConnection())
    {
        var result =
            await connection.QueryAsync<Icecream>(query);
        return result.ToList();
    }
}
```

Let's try to understand all the steps in this method. We created a string called `query`, where we store the SQL query to fetch all the entities from the database.

Then, inside the `using` statement, we used `DapperContext` to create the connection.

Once the connection was created, we used it to call the `QueryAsync` method and passed the query as an argument.

Dapper, when the results return from the database, converted them into `IEnumerable<T>` automatically.

The following is the final code of the interface and our first implementation:

```
public interface IIcecreamsRepository
{
    public Task<IEnumerable<Icecream>> GetIcecreams();
}

public class IcecreamsRepository : IIcecreamsRepository
{
    private readonly DapperContext _context;
    public IcecreamsRepository(DapperContext context)
    {
        _context = context;
    }

    public async Task<IEnumerable<Icecream>> GetIcecreams()
    {
        var query = "SELECT * FROM Icecreams";
        using (var connection =
            _context.CreateConnection())
        {
            var result =
                await connection.QueryAsync<Icecream>(query);
            return result.ToList();
        }
    }
}
```

In the next section, we will see how to add a new entity to the database and how to use the ExecuteAsync method to run a query.

Adding a new entity in the database with Dapper

Now we are going to manage adding a new entity to the database for future implementations of the API post request.

Let's modify the interface by adding a new method called `CreateIcecream` with an input parameter of the `Icecream` type:

```
public Task CreateIcecream(Icecream icecream);
```

Now we must implement this method in the repository class:

```
public async Task CreateIcecream(Icecream icecream)
{
    var query = "INSERT INTO Icecreams (Name, Description)
      VALUES (@Name, @Description)";
    var parameters = new DynamicParameters();
    parameters.Add("Name", icecream.Name, DbType.String);
    parameters.Add("Description", icecream.Description,
                    DbType.String);
    using (var connection = _context.CreateConnection())
    {
        await connection.ExecuteAsync(query, parameters);
    }
}
```

Here, we create the query and a dynamic parameters object to pass all the values to the database.

We populate the parameters with the values from the `Icecream` object in the method parameter.

We create the connection with the Dapper context and then we use the `ExecuteAsync` method to execute the `INSERT` statement.

This method returns an integer value as a result, representing the number of affected rows in the database. In this case, we don't use this information, but you can return this value as the result of the method if you need it.

Implementing the repository in the endpoints

To add the final touch to our minimal API, we need to implement the two endpoints to manage all the methods in our repository pattern:

```
app.MapPost("/icecreams", async (IIcecreamsRepository
repository, Icecream icecream) =>
{
    await repository.CreateIcecream(icecream);
    return Results.Ok();
});
app.MapGet("/icecreams", async (IIcecreamsRepository
repository) => await repository.GetIcecreams());
```

In both map methods, we pass the repository as a parameter because, as usual in the minimal API, the services are passed as parameters in the map methods.

This means that the repository is always available in all parts of the code.

In the `MapGet` endpoint, we use the repository to load all the entities from the implementation of the repository and we use the result as the result of the endpoint.

In the `MapPost` endpoint, in addition to the repository parameter, we accept also the `Icecream` entity from the body of the request and we use the same entity as a parameter to the `CreateIcecream` method of the repository.

Summary

In this chapter, we learned how to interact with a data access layer in a minimal API project with the two most common tools in a real-world scenario: EF and Dapper.

For EF, we covered some basic features, such as setting up a project to use this ORM and how to perform some basic operations to implement a full CRUD API endpoint.

We did basically the same thing with Dapper as well, starting from an empty project, adding Dapper, setting up the project for working with a SQL Server LocalDB, and implementing some basic interactions with the entities of the database.

In the next chapter, we'll focus on authentication and authorization in a minimal API project. It's important, first of all, to protect your data in the database.

Part 3:
Advanced Development and Microservices Concepts

In this advanced section of the book, we want to show more scenarios that are typical in backend development. We will also go over the performance of this new framework and understand the scenarios in which it is really useful.

We will cover the following chapters in this section:

- *Chapter 8, Adding Authentication and Authorization*
- *Chapter 9, Leveraging Globalization and Localization*
- *Chapter 10, Evaluating and Benchmarking the Performance of Minimal APIs*

8

Adding Authentication and Authorization

Any kind of application must deal with **authentication** and **authorization**. Often, these terms are used interchangeably, but they actually refer to different scenarios. In this chapter of the book, we will explain the difference between authentication and authorization and show how to add these features to a minimal API project.

Authentication can be performed in many different ways: using local accounts with external login providers, such as Microsoft, Google, Facebook, and Twitter; using Azure Active Directory and Azure B2C; and using authentication servers such as Identity Server and Okta. Moreover, we may have to deal with requirements such as two-factor authentication and refresh tokens. In this chapter, however, we will focus on the general aspects of authentication and authorization and see how to implement them in a minimal API project, in order to provide a general understanding of the topic. The information and samples that will be provided will show how to effectively work with authentication and authorization and how to customize their behaviors according to our requirements.

In this chapter, we will be covering the following topics:

- Introducing authentication and authorization
- Protecting a minimal API
- Handling authorization – roles and policies

Technical requirements

To follow the examples in this chapter, you will need to create an ASP.NET Core 6.0 Web API application. Refer to the *Technical requirements* section in *Chapter 2, Exploring Minimal APIs and Their Advantages*, for instructions on how to do so.

If you're using your console, shell, or Bash terminal to create the API, remember to change your working directory to the current chapter number: Chapter08.

All the code samples in this chapter can be found in the GitHub repository for this book at `https://github.com/PacktPublishing/Minimal-APIs-in-ASP.NET-Core-6/tree/main/Chapter08`.

Introducing authentication and authorization

As said at the beginning, the terms authentication and authorization are often used interchangeably, but they represent different security functions. Authentication is the process of verifying that users are who they say they are, while authorization is the task of granting an authenticated user permission to do something. So, authorization must always follow authentication.

Let's think about the security in an airport: first, you show your ID to authenticate your identity; then, at the gate, you present the boarding pass to be authorized to board the flight and get access to the plane.

Authentication and authorization in ASP.NET Core are handled by corresponding middleware and work in the same way in minimal APIs and controller-based projects. They allow the restriction of access to endpoints depending on user identity, roles, policies, and so on, as we'll see in detail in the following sections.

You can find a great overview of ASP.NET Core authentication and authorization in the official documentation available at `https://docs.microsoft.com/aspnet/core/security/authentication` and `https://docs.microsoft.com/aspnet/core/security/authorization`.

Protecting a minimal API

Protecting a minimal API means correctly setting up authentication and authorization. There are many types of authentication solutions that are adopted in modern applications. In web applications, we typically use cookies, while when dealing with web APIs, we use methods such as an API key, basic authentication, and **JSON Web Token** (**JWT**). JWTs are the most commonly used, and in the rest of the chapter, we'll focus on this solution.

> **Note**
> A good starting point to understand what JWTs are and how they are used is available at `https://jwt.io/introduction`.

To enable authentication and authorization based on JWT, the first thing to do is to add the `Microsoft.AspNetCore.Authentication.JwtBearer` NuGet package to our project, using one of the following ways:

- **Option 1**: If you're using Visual Studio 2022, right-click on the project and choose the **Manage NuGet Packages** command to open **Package Manager GUI**, then search for `Microsoft.AspNetCore.Authentication.JwtBearer` and click on **Install**.

- **Option 2**: Open **Package Manager Console** if you're inside Visual Studio 2022, or open your console, shell, or Bash terminal, go to your project directory, and execute the following command:

```
dotnet add package Microsoft.AspNetCore.Authentication.
JwtBearer
```

Now, we need to add authentication and authorization services to the service provider, so that they are available through dependency injection:

```
var builder = WebApplication.CreateBuilder(args);
//...
builder.Services.AddAuthentication(JwtBearerDefaults.
AuthenticationScheme).AddJwtBearer();
builder.Services.AddAuthorization();
```

This is the minimum code that is necessary to add JWT authentication and authorization support to an ASP.NET Core project. It isn't a real working solution yet, because it is missing the actual configuration, but it is enough to verify how endpoint protection works.

In the `AddAuthentication()` method, we specify that we want to use the **bearer authentication scheme**. This is an HTTP authentication scheme that involves security tokens that are in fact called **bearer tokens**. These tokens must be sent in the `Authorization` HTTP header with the format `Authorization: Bearer <token>`. Then, we call `AddJwtBearer()` to tell ASP.NET Core that it must expect a bearer token in the JWT format. As we'll see later, the bearer token is an encoded string generated by the server in response to a login request. After that, we use `AddAuthorization()` to also add authorization services.

Now, we need to insert authentication and authorization middleware in the pipeline so that ASP.NET Core will be instructed to check the token and apply all the authorization rules:

```
var app = builder.Build();
//..

app.UseAuthentication();
app.UseAuthorization();
```

```
//...
app.Run();
```

> **Important Note**
>
> We have said that authorization must follow authentication. This means that the authentication middleware must come first; otherwise, the security will not work as expected.

Finally, we can protect our endpoints using the `Authorize` attribute or the `RequireAuthorization()` method:

```
app.MapGet("/api/attribute-protected", [Authorize] () => "This
endpoint is protected using the Authorize attribute");

app.MapGet("/api/method-protected", () => "This endpoint is
protected using the RequireAuthorization method")
.RequireAuthorization();
```

> **Note**
>
> The ability to specify an attribute directly on a lambda expression (as in the first endpoint of the previous example) is a new feature of C# 10.

If we now try to call each of these methods using Swagger, we'll get a `401 unauthorized` response, which should look as follows:

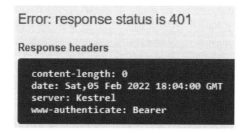

Figure 8.1 – Unauthorized response in Swagger

Note that the message contains a header indicating that the expected authentication scheme is `Bearer`, as we have declared in the code.

So, now we know how to restrict access to our endpoints to authenticated users. But our work isn't finished: we need to generate a JWT bearer, validate it, and find a way to pass such a token to Swagger so that we can test our protected endpoints.

Generating a JWT bearer

We have said that a JWT bearer is generated by the server as a response to a login request. ASP.NET Core provides all the APIs we need to create it, so let's see how to perform this task.

The first thing to do is to define the login request endpoint to authenticate the user with their username and password:

```
app.MapPost("/api/auth/login", (LoginRequest request) =>
{
    if (request.Username == "marco" && request.Password ==
        "P@$$w0rd")
    {
        // Generate the JWT bearer...
    }

    return Results.BadRequest();
});
```

For the sake of simplicity, in the preceding example, we have used hardcoded values, but in a real application, we'd use, for example, **ASP.NET Core Identity**, the part of ASP.NET Core that is responsible for user management. More information on this topic is available in the official documentation at `https://docs.microsoft.com/aspnet/core/security/authentication/identity`.

In a typical login workflow, if the credentials are invalid, we return a `400 Bad Request` response to the client. If, instead, the username and password are correct, we can effectively generate a JWT bearer, using the classes available in ASP.NET Core:

```
var claims = new List<Claim>()
{
    new(ClaimTypes.Name, request.Username)
};

var securityKey = new SymmetricSecurityKey(Encoding.UTF8.
GetBytes("mysecuritystring"));
var credentials = new SigningCredentials(securityKey,
SecurityAlgorithms.HmacSha256);

var jwtSecurityToken = new JwtSecurityToken(
    issuer: "https://www.packtpub.com",
```

```
        audience: "Minimal APIs Client",
        claims: claims, expires: DateTime.UtcNow.AddHours(1),
           signingCredentials: credentials);


    var accessToken = new JwtSecurityTokenHandler()
       .WriteToken(jwtSecurityToken);


    return Results.Ok(new { AccessToken = accessToken });
```

JWT bearer creation involves many different concepts, but through the preceding code example, we'll focus on the basic ones. This kind of bearer contains information that allows verifying the user identity, along with other declarations that describe the properties of the user. These properties are called **claims** and are expressed as string key-value pairs. In the preceding code, we created a list with a single claim that contains the username. We can add as many claims as we need, and we can also have claims with the same name. In the next sections, we'll see how to use claims, for example, to enforce authorization.

Next in the preceding code, we defined the credentials (`SigningCredentials`) to sign the JWT bearer. The signature depends on the actual token content and is used to check that the token hasn't been tampered with. In fact, if we change anything in the token, such as a claim value, the signature will consequentially change. As the key to sign the bearer is known only by the server, it is impossible for a third party to modify the token and sustain its validity. In the preceding code, we used `SymmetricSecurityKey`, which is never shared with clients.

We used a short string to create the credentials, but the only requirement is that the key should be at least 32 bytes or 16 characters long. In .NET, strings are Unicode and therefore, each character takes 2 bytes. We also needed to set the algorithm that the credentials will use to sign the token. To this end, we have specified the **Hash-Based Message Authentication Code (HMAC)** and the hash function, SHA256, specifying the `SecurityAlgorithms.HmacSha256` value. This algorithm is quite a common choice in these kinds of scenarios.

> **Note**
>
> You can find more information about the HMAC and the SHA256 hash function at `https://docs.microsoft.com/dotnet/api/system.security.cryptography.hmacsha256#remarks`.

By this point in the preceding code, we finally have all the information to create the token, so we can instantiate a `JwtSecurityToken` object. This class can use many parameters to build the token, but for the sake of simplicity, we have specified only the minimum set for a working example:

- **Issuer**: A string (typically a URI) that identifies the name of the entity that is creating the token
- **Audience**: The recipient that the JWT is intended for, that is, who can consume the token
- The list of claims
- The expiration time of the token (in UTC)
- The signing credentials

> **Tip**
>
> In the preceding code example, values used to build the token are hardcoded, but in a real-life application, we should place them in an external source, for example, in the `appsettings.json` configuration file.

You can find further information on creating a token at `https://docs.microsoft.com/dotnet/api/system.identitymodel.tokens.jwt.jwtsecuritytoken`.

After all the preceding steps, we could create `JwtSecurityTokenHandler`, which is responsible for actually generating the bearer token and returning it to the caller with a `200 OK` response.

So, now we can try the `login` endpoint in Swagger. After inserting the correct username and password and clicking the **Execute** button, we will get the following response:

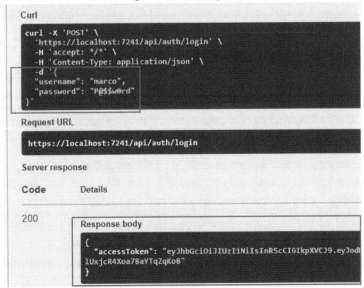

Figure 8.2 – The JWT bearer as a result of the login request in Swagger

We can copy the token value and insert it in the URL of the site `https://jwt.ms` to see what it contains. We'll get something like this:

```
{
  "alg": "HS256",
  "typ": "JWT"
}.{
  "http://schemas.xmlsoap.org/ws/2005/05/identity/claims/name":
"marco",
  "exp": 1644431527,
  "iss": "https://www.packtpub.com",
  "aud": "Minimal APIs Client"
}.[Signature]
```

In particular, we see the claims that have been configured:

- name: The name of the logged user

- exp: The token expiration time, expressed in Unix epoch

- iss: The issuer of the token

- aud: The audience (receiver) of the token

This is the raw view, but we can switch to the **Claims** tab to see the decoded list of all the claims, with a description of their meaning, where available.

There is one important point that requires attention: by default, the JWT bearer isn't encrypted (it's just a Base64-encoded string), so everyone can read its content. Token security does not depend on the inability to be decoded, but on the fact that it is signed. Even if the token's content is clear, it is impossible to modify it because in this case, the signature (which uses a key that is known only by the server) will become invalid.

So, it's important not to insert sensitive data in the token; claims such as usernames, user IDs, and roles are usually fine, but, for example, we should not insert information related to privacy. To give a deliberately exaggerated example, we mustn't insert a credit card number in the token! In any case, keep in mind that even Microsoft for Azure Active Directory uses JWT, with no encryption, so we can trust this security system.

In conclusion, we have described how to obtain a valid JWT. The next steps are to pass the token to our protected endpoints and instruct our minimal API on how to validate it.

Validating a JWT bearer

After creating the JWT bearer, we need to pass it in every HTTP request, inside the `Authorization` HTTP header, so that ASP.NET Core can verify its validity and allow us to invoke the protected endpoints. So, we have to complete the `AddJwtBearer()` method invocation that we showed earlier with the description of the rules to validate the bearer:

```
builder.Services.AddAuthentication(JwtBearerDefaults.
AuthenticationScheme)
.AddJwtBearer(options =>
{
    options.TokenValidationParameters = new
TokenValidationParameters
    {
        ValidateIssuerSigningKey = true,
        IssuerSigningKey = new SymmetricSecurityKey(
          Encoding.UTF8.GetBytes("mysecuritystring")),
        ValidIssuer = "https://www.packtpub.com",
        ValidAudience = "Minimal APIs Client"
    };
});
```

In the preceding code, we added a lambda expression with which we defined the `TokenValidationParameter` object that contains the token validation rules. First of all, we checked the issuer signing key, that is, the signature of the token, as shown in the *Generating a JWT bearer* section, to verify that the JWT has not been tampered with. The security string that has been used to sign the token is required to perform this check, so we specify the same value (`mysecuritystring`) that we inserted during the login request.

Then, we specify what valid values for the issuer and the audience of the token are. If the token has been emitted from a different issuer, or was intended for another audience, the validation fails. This is an important security check; we should be sure that the bearer has been issued by someone we expected to issue it and for the audience we want.

> **Tip**
>
> As already pointed out, we should place the information used to work with the token in an external source, so that we can reference the correct values during token generation and validation, avoiding hardcoding them or writing their values twice.

We don't need to specify that we also want to validate the token expiration because this check is automatically enabled. A clock skew is applied when validating the time to compensate for slight differences in clock time or to handle delays between the client request and the instant at which it is processed by the server. The default value is 5 minutes, which means that an expired token is considered valid for a 5-minute timeframe after its actual expiration. We can reduce the clock skew, or disable it, using the `ClockSkew` property of the `TokenValidationParameter` class.

Now, the minimal API has all the information to check the bearer token validity. In order to test whether everything works as expected, we need a way to tell Swagger how to send the token within a request, as we'll see in the next section.

Adding JWT support to Swagger

We have said that the bearer token is sent in the `Authorization` HTTP header of a request. If we want to use Swagger to verify the authentication system and test our protected endpoints, we need to update the configuration so that it will be able to include this header in the requests.

To perform this task, it is necessary to add a bit of code to the `AddSwaggerGen()` method:

```
var builder = WebApplication.CreateBuilder(args);
//...

builder.Services.AddSwaggerGen(options =>
{
    options.AddSecurityDefinition(JwtBearerDefaults.
AuthenticationScheme, new OpenApiSecurityScheme
    {
        Type = SecuritySchemeType.ApiKey,
        In = ParameterLocation.Header,
        Name = HeaderNames.Authorization,
        Description = "Insert the token with the 'Bearer '
                        prefix"
    });

    options.AddSecurityRequirement(new
      OpenApiSecurityRequirement
    {
        {
            new OpenApiSecurityScheme
            {
```

```
                    Reference = new OpenApiReference
                    {
                        Type = ReferenceType.SecurityScheme,
                        Id =
                        JwtBearerDefaults.AuthenticationScheme
                    }
                },
                Array.Empty<string>()
            }
        });
    });
```

In the preceding code, we defined how Swagger handles authentication. Using the `AddSecurityDefinition()` method, we described how our API is protected; we used an API key, which is the bearer token, in the header with the name `Authorization`. Then, with `AddSecurityRequirement()`, we specified that we have a security requirement for our endpoints, which means that the security information must be sent for every request.

After adding the preceding code, if we now run our application, the Swagger UI will contain something new.

Figure 8.3 – Swagger showing the authentication features

Upon clicking the **Authorize** button or any of the padlock icons at the right of the endpoints, the following window will show up, allowing us to insert the bearer token:

Figure 8.4 – The window that allows setting the bearer token

The last thing to do is to insert the token in the **Value** textbox and confirm by clicking on **Authorize**. From now on, the specified bearer will be sent along with every request made with Swagger.

We have finally completed all the required steps to add authentication support to minimal APIs. Now, it's time to verify that everything works as expected. In the next section, we'll perform some tests.

Testing authentication

As described in the previous sections, if we call one of the protected endpoints, we get a 401 Unauthorized response. To verify that token authentication works, let's call the login endpoint to get a token. After that, click on the **Authorize** button in Swagger and insert the obtained token, remembering the Bearer<space> prefix. Now, we'll get a 200 OK response, meaning that we are able to correctly invoke the endpoints that require authentication. We can also try changing a single character in the token to again get the 401 Unauthorized response, because in this case, the signature will not be the expected one, as described before. In the same way, if the token is formally valid but has expired, we will obtain a 401 response.

As we have defined endpoints that can be reached only by authenticated users, a common requirement is to access user information within the corresponding route handlers. In *Chapter 2, Exploring Minimal APIs and Their Advantages*, we showed that minimal APIs provide a special binding that directly provides a ClaimsPrincipal object representing the logged user:

```
app.MapGet("/api/me", [Authorize] (ClaimsPrincipal user) =>
$"Logged username: {user.Identity.Name}");
```

The `user` parameter of the route handler is automatically filled with user information. In this example, we just get the name, which in turn is read from the token claims, but the object exposes many properties that allow us to work with authentication data. We can refer to the official documentation at `https://docs.microsoft.com/dotnet/api/system.security.claims.claimsprincipal.identity` for further details.

This ends our overview of authentication. In the next section, we'll see how to handle authorization.

Handling authorization – roles and policies

Right after the authentication, there is the authorization step, which grants an authenticated user permission to do something. Minimal APIs provide the same authorization features as controller-based projects, based on the concepts of **roles** and **policies**.

When an identity is created, it may belong to one or more roles. For example, a user can belong to the `Administrator` role, while another can be part of two roles: `User` and `Stakeholder`. Typically, each user can perform only the operations that are allowed by their roles. Roles are just claims that are inserted in the JWT bearer upon authentication. As we'll see in a moment, ASP.NET Core provides built-in support to verify whether a user belongs to a role.

While role-based authorization covers many scenarios, there are cases in which this kind of security isn't enough because we need to apply more specific rules to check whether the user has the right to perform some activities. In such a situation, we can create custom policies that allow us to specify more detailed authorization requirements and even completely define the authorization logic based on our algorithms.

In the next sections, we'll see how to manage both role-based and policy-based authorization in our APIs, so that we can cover all our requirements, that is, allowing access to certain endpoints only to users with specific roles or claims, or based on our custom logic.

Handling role-based authorization

As already introduced, roles are claims. This means that they must be inserted in the JWT bearer token upon authentication, just like any other claims:

```
app.MapPost("/api/auth/login", (LoginRequest request) =>
{
    if (request.Username == "marco" && request.Password ==
        "P@$$w0rd")
    {
        var claims = new List<Claim>()
        {
            new(ClaimTypes.Name, request.Username),
```

```
            new(ClaimTypes.Role, "Administrator"),
            new(ClaimTypes.Role, "User")
        };


    //...
}
```

In this example, we statically add two claims with name `ClaimTypes.Role`: `Administrator` and `User`. As said in the previous sections, in a real-world application, these values typically come from a complete user management system built, for example, with ASP.NET Core Identity.

As in all the other claims, roles are inserted in the JWT bearer. If now we try to invoke the `login` endpoint, we'll notice that the token is longer because it contains a lot of information, which we can verify using the `https://jwt.ms` site again, as follows:

```
{
    "alg": "HS256",
    "typ": "JWT"
}.{
    "http://schemas.xmlsoap.org/ws/2005/05/identity/claims/name":
"marco",
    "http://schemas.microsoft.com/ws/2008/06/identity/claims/
role": [
        "Administrator",
        "User"
    ],
    "exp": 1644755166,
    "iss": "https://www.packtpub.com",
    "aud": "Minimal APIs Client"
}.[Signature]
```

In order to restrict access to a particular endpoint only for users that belong to a given role, we need to specify this role as an argument in the `Authorize` attribute or the `RequireAuthorization()` method:

```
app.MapGet("/api/admin-attribute-protected", [Authorize(Roles =
"Administrator")] () => { });


app.MapGet("/api/admin-method-protected", () => { })
```

```
.RequireAuthorization(new AuthorizeAttribute { Roles =
"Administrator" });
```

In this way, only users who are assigned the Administrator role can access the endpoints. We can also specify more roles, separating them with a comma: the user will be authorized if they have at least one of the specified roles.

> **Important Note**
>
> Role names are case sensitive.

Now suppose we have the following endpoint:

```
app.MapGet("/api/stackeholder-protected", [Authorize(Roles =
"Stakeholder")] () => { });
```

This method can only be consumed by a user who is assigned the Stakeholder role. However, in our example, this role isn't assigned. So, if we use the previous bearer token and try to invoke this endpoint, of course, we'll get an error. But in this case, it won't be 401 Unauthorized, but rather 403 Forbidden. We see this behavior because the user is actually authenticated (meaning the token is valid, so no 401 error), but they don't have the authorization to execute the method, so access is forbidden. In other words, authentication errors and authorization errors lead to different HTTP status codes.

There is another important scenario that involves roles. Sometimes, we don't need to restrict endpoint access at all but need to adapt the behavior of the handler according to the specific user role, such as when retrieving only a certain type of information. In this case, we can use the IsInRole() method, which is available on the ClaimsPrincipal object:

```
app.MapGet("/api/role-check", [Authorize] (ClaimsPrincipal
user) =>
{
    if (user.IsInRole("Administrator"))
    {
        return "User is an Administrator";
    }

    return "This is a normal user";
});
```

In this endpoint, we only use the `Authorize` attribute to check whether the user is authenticated or not. Then, in the route handler, we check whether the user has the `Administrator` role. If yes, we just return a message, but we can imagine that administrators can retrieve all the available information, while normal users get only a subset, based on the values of the information itself.

As we have seen, with role-based authorization, we can perform different types of authorization checks in our endpoints, to cover many scenarios. However, this approach cannot handle all situations. If roles aren't enough, we need to use authorization based on policies, which we will discuss in the next section.

Applying policy-based authorization

Policies are a more general way to define authorization rules. Role-based authorization can be considered a specific policy authorization that involves a roles check. We typically use policies when we need to handle more complex scenarios.

This kind of authorization requires two steps:

1. Defining a policy with a rule set
2. Applying a certain policy on the endpoints

Policies are added in the context of the `AddAuthorization()` method, which we saw in the previous section, *Protecting a minimal API*. Each policy has a unique name, which is used to later reference it, and a set of rules, which are typically described in a fluent manner.

We can use policies when role authorization is not enough. Suppose that the bearer token also contains the ID of the tenant to which the user belongs:

```
var claims = new List<Claim>()
{
    // ...
    new("tenant-id", "42")
};
```

Again, in a real-world scenario, this value could come from a database that stores the properties of the user. Suppose that we want to only allow users who belong to a particular tenant to reach an endpoint. As `tenant-id` is a custom claim, ASP.NET Core doesn't know how to use it to enforce authorization. So, we can't use the solutions shown earlier. We need to define a custom policy with the corresponding rule:

```
builder.Services.AddAuthorization(options =>
{
    options.AddPolicy("Tenant42", policy =>
    {
```

```
        policy.RequireClaim("tenant-id", "42");
    });
});
```

In the preceding code, we created a policy named `Tenant42`, which requires that the token contains the `tenant-id` claim with the value `42`. The `policy` variable is an instance of `AuthorizationPolicyBuilder` and exposes methods that allow us to fluently specify the authorization rules; we can specify that a policy requires certain users, roles, and claims to be satisfied. We can also chain multiple requirements in the same policy, writing, for example, something such as `policy.RequireRole("Administrator").RequireClaim("tenant-id")`. The full list of methods is available on the documentation page at `https://docs.microsoft.com/dotnet/api/microsoft.aspnetcore.authorization.authorizationpolicybuilder`.

Then, in the method we want to protect, we have to specify the policy name, as usual with the `Authorize` attribute or the `RequireAuthorization()` method:

```
app.MapGet("/api/policy-attribute-protected", [Authorize(Policy
= "Tenant42")] () => { });

app.MapGet("/api/policy-method-protected", () => { })
.RequireAuthorization("Tenant42");
```

If we try to execute these preceding endpoints with a token that doesn't have the `tenant-id` claim, or its value isn't `42`, we get a `403 Forbidden` result, as happened with the role check.

There are scenarios in which declaring a list of allowed roles and claims isn't enough: for example, we would need to perform more complex checks or verify authorization based on dynamic parameters. In these cases, we can use the so-called **policy requirements**, which comprise a collection of authorization rules for which we can provide custom verification logic.

To adopt this solution, we need two objects:

- A *requirement class* that implements the `IAuthorizationRequirement` interface and defines the requirement we want to manage

- A *handler class* that inherits from `AuthorizationHandler` and contains the logic to verify the requirement

Let's suppose we don't want users who don't belong to the `Administrator` role to access certain endpoints during a maintenance time window. This is a perfectly valid authorization rule, but we cannot afford it using the solutions we have seen up to now. The rule involves a condition that considers the current time, so the policy cannot be statically defined.

So, we start by creating a custom requirement:

```
public class MaintenanceTimeRequirement :
IAuthorizationRequirement
{
    public TimeOnly StartTime { get; init; }

    public TimeOnly EndTime { get; init; }
}
```

The requirement contains the start and end times of the maintenance window. During this interval, we only want administrators to be able to operate.

> **Note**
>
> TimeOnly is a new data type that has been introduced with C# 10 and allows us to store only only the time of the day (and not the date). More information is available at https://docs. microsoft.com/dotnet/api/system.timeonly.

Note that the IAuthorizationRequirement interface is just a placeholder. It doesn't contain any method or property to be implemented; it serves only to identify that the class is a requirement. In other words, if we don't need any additional information for the requirement, we can create a class that implements IAuthorizationRequirement but actually has no content at all.

This requirement must be enforced, so it is necessary to create the corresponding handler:

```
public class MaintenanceTimeAuthorizationHandler
    : AuthorizationHandler<MaintenanceTimeRequirement>
{
    protected override Task HandleRequirementAsync(
        AuthorizationHandlerContext context,
        MaintenanceTimeRequirement requirement)
    {
        var isAuthorized = true;
        if (!context.User.IsInRole("Administrator"))
        {
            var time = TimeOnly.FromDateTime(DateTime.Now);
            if (time >= requirement.StartTime && time <
                requirement.EndTime)
            {
```

```
                    isAuthorized = false;
            }
        }

        if (isAuthorized)
        {
            context.Succeed(requirement);
        }

        return Task.CompletedTask;
    }
}
```

Our handler inherits from `AuthorizationHandler<MaintenanceTimeRequirement>`, so we need to override the `HandleRequirementAsync()` method to verify the requirement, using the `AuthorizationHandlerContext` parameter, which contains a reference to the current user. As said at the beginning, if the user is not assigned the `Administrator` role, we check whether the current time falls in the maintenance window. If so, the user doesn't have the right to access.

At the end, if the `isAuthorized` variable is `true`, it means that the authorization can be granted, so we call the `Succeed()` method on the `context` object, passing the requirement that we want to validate. Otherwise, we don't invoke any method on the context, meaning that the requirement hasn't been verified.

We haven't yet finished implementing the custom policy. We still have to define the policy and register the handler in the service provider:

```
builder.Services.AddAuthorization(options =>
{
    options.AddPolicy("TimedAccessPolicy", policy =>
    {
        policy.Requirements.Add(new
          MaintenanceTimeRequirement
        {
            StartTime = new TimeOnly(0, 0, 0),
            EndTime = new TimeOnly(4, 0, 0)
        });
    });
});
```

```
});


builder.Services.AddScoped<IAuthorizationHandler,
MaintenanceTimeAuthorizationHandler>();
```

In the preceding code, we defined a maintenance time window from midnight till 4:00 in the morning. Then, we registered the handler as an implementation of the `IAuthorizationHandler` interface, which in turn is implemented by the `AuthorizationHandler` class.

Now that we have everything in place, we can apply the policy to our endpoints:

```
app.MapGet("/api/custom-policy-protected", [Authorize(Policy =
"TimedAccessPolicy")] () => { });
```

When we try to reach this endpoint, ASP.NET Core will check the corresponding policy, find that it contains a requirement, and scan all the registrations of the `IAuhorizationHandler` interface to see whether there is one that is able to handle the requirement. Then, the handler will be invoked, and the result will be used to determine whether the user has the right to access the route. If the policy isn't verified, we'll get a `403 Forbidden` response.

We have shown how powerful policies are, but there is more. We can also use them to define global rules that are automatically applied to all endpoints, using the concepts of default and fallback policies, as we'll see in the next section.

Using default and fallback policies

Default and fallback policies are useful when we want to define global rules that must be automatically applied. In fact, when we use the `Authorize` attribute or the `RequireAuthorization()` method, without any other parameter, we implicitly refer to the default policy defined by ASP.NET Core, which is set to require an authenticated user.

If we want to use different conditions by default, we just need to redefine the `DefaultPolicy` property, which is available in the context of the `AddAuthorization()` method:

```
builder.Services.AddAuthorization(options =>
{
    var policy = new AuthorizationPolicyBuilder()
      .RequireAuthenticatedUser()
        .RequireClaim("tenant-id").Build();

    options.DefaultPolicy = policy;
});
```

We use `AuthorizationPolicyBuilder` to define all the security requirements, then we set it as a default policy. In this way, even if we don't specify a custom policy in the `Authorize` attribute or the `RequireAuthorization()` method, the system will always verify whether the user is authenticated, and the bearer contains the `tenant-id` claim. Of course, we can override this default behavior by just specifying roles or policy names in the authorization attribute or method.

A fallback policy, on the other hand, is the policy that is applied when there is no authorization information on the endpoints. It is useful, for example, when we want all our endpoints to be automatically protected, even if we forget to specify the `Authorize` attribute or just don't want to repeat the attribute for each handler. Let us try and understand this using the following code:

```
builder.Services.AddAuthorization(options =>
{
    options.FallbackPolicy = options.DefaultPolicy;
});
```

In the preceding code, `FallbackPolicy` becomes equal to `DefaultPolicy`. We have said that the default policy requires that the user be authenticated, so the result of this code is that now, all the endpoints automatically need authentication, even if we don't explicitly protect them.

This is a typical solution to adopt when most of our endpoints have restricted access. We don't need to specify the `Authorize` attribute or use the `RequireAuthorization()` method anymore. In other words, now all our endpoints are protected by default.

If we decide to use this approach, but a bunch of endpoints need public access, such as the `login` endpoint, which everyone should be able to invoke, we can use the `AllowAnonymous` attribute or the `AllowAnonymous()` method:

```
app.MapPost("/api/auth/login", [AllowAnonymous] (LoginRequest
request) => { });


// OR


app.MapPost("/api/auth/login", (LoginRequest request) => { })
.AllowAnonymous();
```

As the name implies, the preceding code will bypass all authorization checks for the endpoint, including the default and fallback authorization policies.

To deepen our knowledge of policy-based authentication, we can refer to the official documentation at `https://docs.microsoft.com/aspnet/core/security/authorization/policies`.

Summary

Knowing how authentication and authorization work in minimal APIs is fundamental to developing secure applications. Using JWT bearer authentication roles and policies, we can even define complex authorization scenarios, with the ability to use both standard and custom rules.

In this chapter, we have introduced basic concepts to make a service secure, but there is much more to talk about, especially regarding ASP.NET Core Identity: an API that supports login functionality and allows managing users, passwords, profile data, roles, claims, and more. We can look further into this topic by checking out the official documentation, which is available at `https://docs.microsoft.com/aspnet/core/security/authentication/identity`.

In the next chapter, we will see how to add multilanguage support to our minimal APIs and how to correctly handle applications that work with different date formats, time zones, and so on.

9

Leveraging Globalization and Localization

When developing an application, it is important to think about multi-language support; a multilingual application allows for a wider audience reach. This is also true for web APIs: messages returned by endpoints (for example, validation errors) should be localized, and the service should be able to handle different cultures and deal with time zones. In this chapter of the book, we will talk about **globalization** and **localization**, and we will explain what features are available in minimal APIs to work with these concepts. The information and samples that will be provided will guide us when adding multi-language support to our services and correctly handling all the related behaviors so that we will be able to develop global applications.

In this chapter, we will be covering the following topics:

- Introducing globalization and localization
- Localizing a minimal API application
- Using resource files
- Integrating localization in validation frameworks
- Adding UTC support to a globalized minimal API

Technical requirements

To follow the descriptions in this chapter, you will need to create an ASP.NET Core 6.0 Web API application. Refer to the *Technical requirements* section in *Chapter 1, Introduction to Minimal APIs*, for instructions on how to do so.

If you're using your console, shell, or Bash terminal to create the API, remember to change your working directory to the current chapter number (Chapter09).

All the code samples in this chapter can be found in the GitHub repository for this book at `https://github.com/PacktPublishing/Minimal-APIs-in-ASP.NET-Core-6/tree/main/Chapter09`.

Introducing globalization and localization

When thinking about internationalization, we must deal with globalization and localization, two terms that seem to refer to the same concepts but actually involve different areas. Globalization is the task of designing applications that can manage and support different cultures. Localization is the process of adapting an application to a particular culture, for example, by providing translated resources for each culture that will be supported.

> **Note**
>
> The terms internationalization, globalization, and localization are often abbreviated to *I18N*, *G11N*, and *L10N*, respectively.

As with all the other features that we have already introduced in the previous chapters, globalization and localization can be handled by the corresponding middleware and services that ASP.NET Core provides and work in the same way in minimal APIs and controller-based projects.

You can find a great introduction to globalization and localization in the official documentation available at `https://docs.microsoft.com/dotnet/core/extensions/globalization` and `https://docs.microsoft.com/dotnet/core/extensions/localization`, respectively. In the rest of the chapter, we will focus on how to add support for these features in a minimal API project; in this way, we'll introduce some important concepts and explain how to leverage globalization and localization in ASP.NET Core.

Localizing a minimal API application

To enable localization within a minimal API application, let us go through the following steps:

1. The first step to making an application localizable is to specify the supported cultures by setting the corresponding options, as follows:

    ```
    var builder = WebApplication.CreateBuilder(args);
    //...

    var supportedCultures = new CultureInfo[] { new("en"),
    new("it"), new("fr") };
    builder.Services.
    Configure<RequestLocalizationOptions>(options =>
    ```

```
{
    options.SupportedCultures = supportedCultures;
    options.SupportedUICultures = supportedCultures;
    options.DefaultRequestCulture = new
    RequestCulture(supportedCultures.First());
});
```

In our example, we want to support three cultures – English, Italian, and French – so, we create an array of `CultureInfo` objects.

We're defining neutral cultures, that is, cultures that have a language but are not associated with a country or region. We could also use specific cultures, such as `en-US` or `en-GB`, to represent the cultures of a particular region: for example, `en-US` would refer to the English culture prevalent in the United States, while `en-GB` would refer to the English culture prevalent in the United Kingdom. This difference is important because, depending on the scenario, we may need to use country-specific information to correctly implement localization. For example, if we want to show a date, we have to know that the date format in the United States is `M/d/yyyy`, while in the United Kingdom, it is `dd/MM/yyyy`. So, in this case, it becomes fundamental to work with specific cultures. We also use specific cultures if we need to support language differences across cultures. For example, a particular word may have different spellings depending on the country (e.g., *color* in the US versus *colour* in the UK). That said, for our scenario of minimal APIs, working with neutral cultures is just fine.

2. Next, we configure `RequestLocalizationOptions`, setting the cultures and specifying the default one to use if no information about the culture is provided. We specify both the supported cultures and the supported UI cultures:

   - The supported cultures control the output of culture-dependent functions, such as date, time, and number format.

   - The supported UI cultures are used to choose which translated strings (from `.resx` files) are searched for. We will talk about `.resx` files later in this chapter.

   In a typical application, cultures and UI cultures are set to the same values, but of course, we can use different options if needed.

3. Now that we have configured our service to support globalization, we need to add the localization middleware to the ASP.NET Core pipeline so it will be able to automatically set the culture of the request. Let us do so using the following code:

```
var app = builder.Build();

//...
app.UseRequestLocalization();
```

```
//...

app.Run();
```

In the preceding code, with `UseRequestLocalization()`, we're adding `RequestLocalizationMiddleware` to the ASP.NET Core pipeline to set the current culture of each request. This task is performed using a list of `RequestCultureProvider` that can read information about the culture from various sources. Default providers comprise the following:

- `QueryStringRequestCultureProvider`: Searches for the `culture` and `ui-culture` query string parameters

- `CookieRequestCultureProvider`: Uses the ASP.NET Core cookie

- `AcceptLanguageHeaderRequestProvider`: Reads the requested culture from the `Accept-Language` HTTP header

For each request, the system will try to use these providers in this exact order, until it finds the first one that can determine the culture. If the culture cannot be set, the one specified in the `DefaultRequestCulture` property of `RequestLocalizationOptions` will be used.

If necessary, it is also possible to change the order of the request culture providers or even define a custom provider to implement our own logic to determine the culture. More information on this topic is available at `https://docs.microsoft.com/aspnet/core/fundamentals/localization#use-a-custom-provider`.

> **Important note**
> The localization middleware must be inserted before any other middleware that might use the request culture.

In the case of web APIs, whether using controller-based or minimal APIs, we usually set the request culture through the `Accept-Language` HTTP header. In the following section, we will see how to extend Swagger with the ability to add this header when trying to invoke methods.

Adding globalization support to Swagger

We want Swagger to provide us with a way to specify the Accept-Language HTTP header for each request so that we can test our globalized endpoints. Technically speaking, this means adding an **operation filter** to Swagger that will be able to automatically insert the language header, using the following code:

```
public class AcceptLanguageHeaderOperationFilter :
IOperationFilter
{
    private readonly List<IOpenApiAny>?
    supportedLanguages;

    public AcceptLanguageHeaderOperationFilter
    (IOptions<RequestLocalizationOptions>
    requestLocalizationOptions)
    {
        supportedLanguages =
        requestLocalizationOptions.Value.
        SupportedCultures?.Select(c =>
        newOpenApiString(c.TwoLetterISOLanguageName)).
        Cast<IOpenApiAny>().              ToList();
    }


    public void Apply(OpenApiOperation operation,
    OperationFilterContext context)
    {
        if (supportedLanguages?.Any() ?? false)
        {
            operation.Parameters ??= new
            List<OpenApiParameter>();

            operation.Parameters.Add(new
            OpenApiParameter
            {
                Name = HeaderNames.AcceptLanguage,
                In = ParameterLocation.Header,
```

```
                       Required = false,
                       Schema = new OpenApiSchema
                       {
                              Type = "string",
                              Enum = supportedLanguages,
                              Default = supportedLanguages.
                              First()
                       }
                });
            }
        }
    }
```

In the preceding code, `AcceptLanguageHeaderOperationFilter` takes the `RequestLocalizationOptions` object via dependency injection that we have defined at startup and extracts the supported languages in the format that Swagger expects from it. Then, in the `Apply()` method, we add a new `OpenApiParameter` that corresponds to the `Accept-Language` header. In particular, with the `Schema.Enum` property, we provide the list of supported languages using the values we have extracted in the constructor. This method is invoked for every operation (that is, every endpoint), meaning that the parameter will be automatically added to each of them.

Now, we need to add the new filter to Swagger:

```
var builder = WebApplication.CreateBuilder(args);
//...

builder.Services.AddSwaggerGen(options =>
{
    options.OperationFilter<AcceptLanguageHeaderOperation
    Filter>();
});
```

As we did with the preceding code, for every operation, Swagger will execute the filter, which in turn will add a parameter to specify the language of the request.

So, let's suppose we have the following endpoint:

```
app.MapGet("/culture", () => Thread.CurrentThread.
CurrentCulture.DisplayName);
```

In the preceding handler, we just return the culture of the thread. This method takes no parameter; however, after adding the preceding filter, the Swagger UI will show the following:

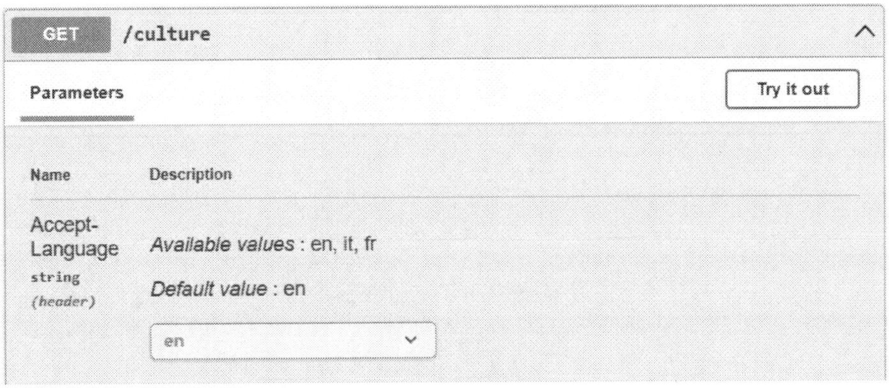

Figure 9.1 – The Accept-Language header added to Swagger

The operation filter has added a new parameter to the endpoint, allowing us to select the language from a dropdown. We can click the **Try it out** button to choose a value from the list and then click **Execute** to invoke the endpoint:

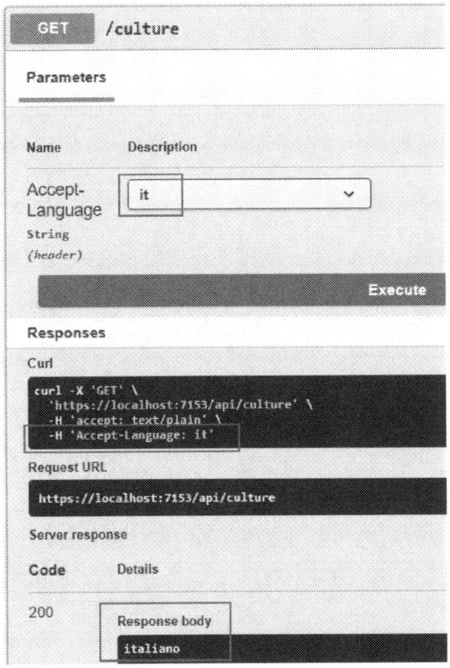

Figure 9.2 – The result of the execution with the Accept-Language HTTP header

This is the result of selecting `it` as a language request: Swagger has added the `Accept-Language` HTTP header, which, in turn, has been used by ASP.NET Core to set the current culture. Then, in the end, we get and return the culture display name in the route handler.

This example shows us that we have correctly added globalization support to our minimal API. In the next section, we'll go further and work with localization, starting by providing translated resources to callers based on the corresponding languages.

Using resource files

Our minimal API now supports globalization, so it can switch cultures based on the request. This means that we can provide localized messages to callers, for example, when communicating validation errors. This feature is based on the so-called **resource files** (`.resx`), a particular kind of XML file that contains key-value string pairs representing messages that must be localized.

> **Note**
>
> These resource files are exactly the same as they have been since the early versions of .NET.

Creating and working with resource files

With resource files, we can easily separate strings from code and group them by culture. Typically, resource files are put in a folder called `Resources`. To create a file of this kind using Visual Studio, let us go through the following steps:

> **Important note**
>
> Unfortunately, Visual Studio Code does not provide support for handling `.resx` files. More information about this topic is available at `https://github.com/dotnet/AspNetCore.Docs/issues/2501`.

1. Right-click on the folder in **Solution Explorer** and then choose **Add | New Item**.
2. In the **Add New Item** dialog window, search for `Resources`, select the corresponding template, and name the file, for example, `Messages.resx`:

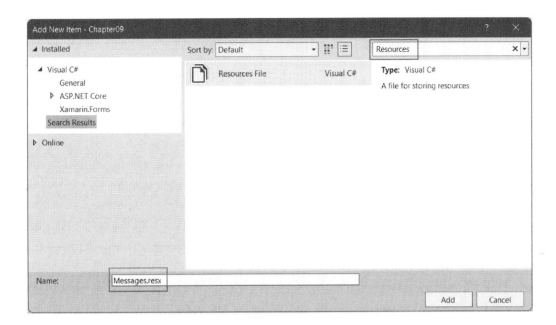

Figure 9.3 – Adding a resource file to the project

The new file will immediately open in the Visual Studio editor.

3.   The first thing to do in the new file is to select **Internal** or **Public** (based on the code visibility we want to achieve) from the **Access Modifier** option so that Visual Studio will create a C# file that exposes the properties to access the resources:

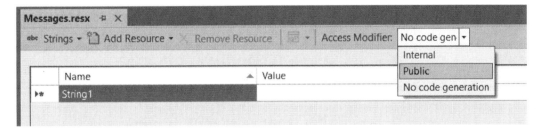

Figure 9.4 – Changing the Access Modifier of the resource file

As soon as we change this value, Visual Studio will add a `Messages.Designer.cs` file to the project and automatically create properties that correspond to the strings we insert in the resource file.

Resource files must follow a precise naming convention. The file that contains default culture messages can have any name (such as Messages.resx, as in our example), but the other .resx files that provide the corresponding translations must have the same name, with the specification of the culture (neutral or specific) to which they refer. So, we have Messages.resx, which will store default (English) messages.

4. Since we also want to localize our messages in Italian, we need to create another file with the name Messages.it.resx.

> **Note**
>
> We don't create a resource file for French culture on purpose because this way, we'll see how APS.NET Core looks up the localized messages in practice.

5. Now, we can start experimenting with resource files. Let's open the Messages.resx file and set **Name** to HelloWorld and **Value** to Hello World!.

    In this way, Visual Studio will add a static HelloWorld property in the Messages autogenerated class that allows us to access values based on the current culture.

6. To demonstrate this behavior, also open the Messages.it.resx file and add an item with the same **Name**, HelloWorld, but now set **Value** to the translation Ciao mondo!.

7. Finally, we can add a new endpoint to showcase the usage of the resource files:

```
// using Chapter09.Resources;
app.MapGet("/helloworld", () => Messages.HelloWorld);
```

In the preceding route handler, we simply access the static Mesasges.HelloWorld property that, as discussed before, has been automatically created while editing the Messages.resx file.

If we now run the minimal API and try to execute this endpoint, we'll get the following responses based on the request language that we select in Swagger:

Accept-Language	Response	Read from
en	Hello World!	Messages.resx
it	Ciao mondo!	Messages.it.resx
fr	Hello World!	Messages.resx

Table 9.1 – Responses based on the request language

When accessing a property such as `HelloWorld`, the autogenerated `Messages` class internally uses `ResourceManager` to look up the corresponding localized string. First of all, it looks for a resource file whose name contains the requested culture. If it is not found, it reverts to the parent culture of that culture. This means that, if the requested culture is specific, `ResourceManager` searches for the neutral culture. If no resource file is still found, then the default one is used.

In our case, using Swagger, we can select only English, Italian, or French as a neutral culture. But what happens if a client sends other values? We can have situations such as the following:

- The request culture is `it-IT`: the system searches for `Messages.it-IT.resx` and then finds and uses `Messages.it.resx`.

- The request culture is `fr-FR`: the system searches for `Messages.fr-FR.resx`, then `Messages.fr.resx`, and (because neither are available) finally uses the default, `Messages.resx`.

- The request culture is `de` (German): because this isn't a supported culture at all, the default request culture will be automatically selected, so strings will be searched for in the `Messages.resx` file.

> **Note**
>
> If a localized resource file exists, but it doesn't contain the specified key, then the value of the default file will be used.

Formatting localized messages using resource files

We can also use resource files to format localized messages. For example, we can add the following strings to the resource files of the project:

Name	Value in Messages.resx	Value in Messages.it.resx
GreetingMessage	Hello, {0}!	Ciao, {0}!

Table 9.2 – A custom localized message

Now, let's define this endpoint:

```
// using Chapter09.Resources;
app.MapGet("/hello", (string name) =>
{
    var message = string.Format(Messages.GreetingMessage,
        name);
```

```
      return message;
});
```

As in the preceding code example, we get a string from a resource file according to the culture of the request. But, in this case, the message contains a placeholder, so we can use it to create a custom localized message using the name that is passed to the route handler. If we try to execute the endpoint, we will get results such as these:

Name	Accept-Language	Response	Read from
Marco	en	Hello, Marco!	Messages.resx
Marco	it	Ciao, Marco!	Messages.it.resx
Marco	fr	Hello, Marco!	Messages.resx

Table 9.3 – Responses with custom localized messages based on the request language

The possibility to create localized messages with placeholders that are replaced at runtime using different values is a key point for creating truly localizable services.

In the beginning, we said that a typical use case of localization in web APIs is when we need to provide localized error messages upon validation. In the next section, we'll see how to add this feature to our minimal API.

Integrating localization in validation frameworks

In *Chapter 6, Exploring Validation and Mapping*, we talked about how to integrate validation into a minimal API project. We learned how to use the MiniValidation library, rather than FluentValidation, to validate our models and provide validation messages to the callers. We also said that FluentValidation already provides translations for standard error messages.

However, with both libraries, we can leverage the localization support we have just added to our project to support localized and custom validation messages.

Localizing validation messages with MiniValidation

Using the MiniValidation library, we can use validation based on **Data Annotations** with minimal APIs. Refer to *Chapter 6, Exploring Validation and Mapping*, for instructions on how to add this library to the project.

Then, recreate the same Person class:

```
public class Person
{
    [Required]
```

```
    [MaxLength(30)]
    public string FirstName { get; set; }


    [Required]
    [MaxLength(30)]
    public string LastName { get; set; }


    [EmailAddress]
    [StringLength(100, MinimumLength = 6)]
    public string Email { get; set; }
}
```

Every validation attribute allows us to specify an error message, which can be a static string or a reference to a resource file. Let's see how to correctly handle the localization for the `Required` attribute. Add the following values in resource files:

Name	Value in Messages.resx	Value in Messages.it.resx
FieldRequiredAnnotation	The field '{0}' is required	Il campo '{0}' è obbligatorio
FirstName	First name	Nome
LastName	Last name	Cognome
ValidationErrors	One or more validation errors occurred.	Si sono verificati errori di validazione.

Table 9.4 – Localized validation error messages used by Data Annotations

We want it so that when a required validation rule fails, the localized message that corresponds to `FieldRequiredAnnotation` is returned. Moreover, this message contains a placeholder, because we want to use it for every required field, so we also need the translation of property names.

With these resources, we can update the `Person` class with the following declarations:

```
public class Person
{
    [Display(Name = "FirstName", ResourceType =
     typeof(Messages))]
    [Required(ErrorMessageResourceName =
    "FieldRequiredAnnotation",
     ErrorMessageResourceType = typeof(Messages))]
```

```
        public string FirstName { get; set; }

        //...
}
```

Each validation attribute, such as `Required` (as used in this example), exposes properties that allow us to specify the name of the resource to use and the type of class that contains the corresponding definition. Keep in mind that the name is a simple string, with no check at compile time, so if we write an incorrect value, we'll only get an error at runtime.

Next, we can use the `Display` attribute to also specify the name of the field that must be inserted in the validation message.

> **Note**
>
> You can find the complete declaration of the `Person` class with localized data annotations on the GitHub repository at `https://github.com/PacktPublishing/Minimal-APIs-in-ASP.NET-Core-6/blob/main/Chapter09/Program.cs#L97`.

Now we can re-add the validation code shown in *Chapter 6, Exploring Validation and Mapping*. The difference is that now the validation messages will be localized:

```
app.MapPost("/people", (Person person) =>
{
    var isValid = MiniValidator.TryValidate(person, out
    var errors);
    if (!isValid)
    {
        return Results.ValidationProblem(errors, title:
        Messages.ValidationErrors);
    }

    return Results.NoContent();
});
```

In the preceding code, the messages contained in the `errors` dictionary that is returned by the `MiniValidator.TryValidate()` method will be localized according to the request culture, as described in the previous sections. We also specify the `title` parameter in the `Results.ValidationProblem()` invocation because we want to localize this value too (otherwise, it will always be the default `One or more validation errors occurred`).

If instead of data annotations, we prefer using `FluentValidation`, we know that it supports localization of standard error messages by default from *Chapter 6, Exploring Validation and Mapping*. However, with this library, we can also provide our translations. In the next section, we'll talk about implementing this solution.

Localizing validation messages with FluentValidation

With `FluentValidation`, we can totally decouple the validation rules from our models. As said before, refer to *Chapter 6, Exploring Validation and Mapping*, for instructions on how to add this library to the project and how to configure it.

Next, let us recreate the `PersonValidator` class:

```
public class PersonValidator : AbstractValidator<Person>
{
    public PersonValidator()
    {
        RuleFor(p => p.FirstName).NotEmpty().
        MaximumLength(30);
        RuleFor(p => p.LastName).NotEmpty().
        MaximumLength(30);
        RuleFor(p => p.Email).EmailAddress().Length(6,
        100);
    }
}
```

In the case that we haven't specified any messages, the default ones will be used. Let's add the following resource to customize the `NotEmpty` validation rule:

Name	Value in Messages.resx	Value in Messages.it.resx
NotEmptyMessage	The field '{PropertyName}' is required	Il campo '{PropertyName}' è obbligatorio

Table 9.5 – The localized validation error messages used by FluentValidation

Note that, in this case, we also have a placeholder that will be replaced by the property name. However, different from data annotations, `FluentValidation` uses a placeholder with a name to better identify its meaning.

Now, we can add this message in the validator, for example, for the `FirstName` property:

```
RuleFor(p => p.FirstName).NotEmpty().
    WithMessage(Messages.NotEmptyMessage).
    WithName(Messages.FirstName);
```

We use `WithMessage()` to specify the message that must be used when the preceding rule fails, following which we add the `WithName()` invocation to overwrite the default property name used for the `{PropertyName}` placeholder of the message.

> **Note**
>
> You can find the complete implementation of the `PersonValidator` class with localized messages in the GitHub repository at `https://github.com/PacktPublishing/Minimal-APIs-in-ASP.NET-Core-6/blob/main/Chapter09/Program.cs#L129`.

Finally, we can leverage the localized validator in our endpoint, as we did in *Chapter 6, Exploring Validation and Mapping*:

```
app.MapPost("/people", async (Person person, IValidator<Person>
validator) =>
{
    var validationResult = await validator.
    ValidateAsync(person);
    if (!validationResult.IsValid)
    {
        var errors = validationResult.ToDictionary();
        return Results.ValidationProblem(errors, title:
        Messages.ValidationErrors);
    }

    return Results.NoContent();
});
```

As in the case of data annotations, the `validationResult` variable will contain localized error messages that we return to the caller using the `Results.ValidationProblem()` method (again, with the definition of the `title` property).

> **Tip**
>
> In our example, we have seen how to explicitly assign translations for each property using the `WithMessage()` method. `FluentValidation` also provides a way to replace all (or some) of its default messages. You can find more information in the official documentation at `https://docs.fluentvalidation.net/en/latest/localization.html#default-messages`.

This ends our overview of localization using resource files. Next, we'll talk about an important topic when dealing with services that are meant to be used worldwide: the correct handling of different time zones.

Adding UTC support to a globalized minimal API

So far, we have added globalization and localization support to our minimal API because we want it to be used by the widest audience possible, irrespective of culture. But, if we think about being accessible to a worldwide audience, we should consider several aspects related to globalization. Globalization does not only pertain to language support; there are important factors we need to consider, for example, geographic locations, as well as time zones.

So, for example, we can have our minimal API running in Italy, which follows *Central European Time* (CET) (GMT+1), while our clients can use browsers that execute a single-page application, rather than mobile apps, all over the world. We could also have a database server that contains our data, and this could be in another time zone. Moreover, at a certain point, it may be necessary to provide better support for worldwide users, so we'll have to move our service to another location, which could have a new time zone. In conclusion, our system could deal with data in different time zones, and, potentially, the same services could switch time zones during their lives.

In these situations, the ideal solution is working with `DateTimeOffset`, a data type that includes time zones and that `JsonSerializer` fully supports, preserving time zone information during serialization and deserialization. If we could always use it, we'd automatically solve any problem related to globalization, because converting a `DateTimeOffset` value to a different time zone is straightforward. However, there are cases in which we can't handle the `DateTimeOffset` type, for example:

- When we're working on a legacy system that relies on `DateTime` everywhere, updating the code to use `DateTimeOffset` isn't an option because it requires too many changes and breaks the compatibility with the old data.

- We have a database server such as MySQL that doesn't have a column type for storing `DateTimeOffset` directly, so handling it requires extra effort, for example, using two separate columns, increasing the complexity of the domain.

- In some cases, we simply aren't interested in sending, receiving, and saving time zones – we just want to handle time in a "universal" way.

So, in all the scenarios where we can't or don't want to use the DateTimeOffset data type, one of the best and simplest ways to deal with different time zones is to handle all dates using *Coordinated Universal Time* (*UTC*): the service must assume that the dates it receives are in the UTC format and, on the other hand, all the dates returned by the API must be in UTC.

Of course, we must handle this behavior in a centralized way; we don't want to have to remember to apply the conversion to and from the UTC format every time we receive or send a date. The well-known JSON.NET library provides an option to specify how to treat the time value when working with a DateTime property, allowing it to automatically handle all dates as UTC and convert them to that format if they represent a local time. However, the current version of Microsoft JsonSerializer used in minimal APIs doesn't include such a feature. From *Chapter 2*, *Exploring Minimal APIs and Their Advantages*, we know that we cannot change the default JSON serializer in minimal APIs, but we can overcome this lack of UTC support by creating a simple JsonConverter:

```
public class UtcDateTimeConverter : JsonConverter<DateTime>
{
    public override DateTime Read(ref Utf8JsonReader
    reader, Type typeToConvert, JsonSerializerOptions
    options)
    => reader.GetDateTime().ToUniversalTime();

    public override void Write(Utf8JsonWriter writer,
    DateTime value, JsonSerializerOptions options)
    => writer.WriteStringValue((value.Kind ==
    DateTimeKind.Local ? value.ToUniversalTime() : value)
    .ToString("yyyy'-'MM'-'dd'T'HH':'mm':'ss'.'
    fffffff'Z'"));
}
```

With this converter, we tell JsonSerializer how to treat DateTime properties:

- When DateTime is read from JSON, the value is converted to UTC using the ToUniversalTime() method.

- When DateTime must be written to JSON, if it represents a local time (DateTimeKind. Local), it is converted to UTC before serialization – then, it is serialized using the Z suffix, which indicates that the time is UTC.

Now, before using this converter, let's add the following endpoint definition:

```
app.MapPost("/date", (DateInput date) =>
{
    return Results.Ok(new
    {
        Input = date.Value,
        DateKind = date.Value.Kind.ToString(),
        ServerDate = DateTime.Now
    });
});


public record DateInput(DateTime Value);
```

Let's try to call it, for example, with a date formatted as `2022-03-06T16:42:37-05:00`. We'll obtain something similar to the following:

```
{
    "input": "2022-03-06T22:42:37+01:00",
    "dateKind": "Local",
    "serverDate": "2022-03-07T18:33:17.0288535+01:00"
}
```

The input date, containing a time zone, has automatically been converted to the local time of the server (in this case, the server is running in Italy, as stated at the beginning), as also demonstrated by the `dateKind` field. Moreover, `serverDate` contains a date that is relative to the server time zone.

Now, let's add `UtcDateTimeConverter` to `JsonSerializer`:

```
var builder = WebApplication.CreateBuilder(args);
//...

builder.Services.Configure<Microsoft.AspNetCore.Http.Json.
JsonOptions>(options =>
{
    options.SerializerOptions.Converters.Add(new
    UtcDateTimeConverter());
});
```

With this configuration, every `DateTime` property will be processed using our custom converters. Now, execute the endpoint again, using the same input as before. This time, the result will be as follows:

```json
{
    "input": "2022-03-06T21:42:37.0000000Z",
    "dateKind": "Utc",
    "serverDate": "2022-03-06T17:40:08.1472051Z"
}
```

The input is the same, but our `UtcDateTimeConverter` has now converted the date to UTC and, on the other hand, has serialized the server date as UTC; now, our API, in a centralized way, can automatically handle all dates as UTC, no matter its time zone or the time zones of the callers.

Finally, there are two other points to make all the systems correctly work with UTC:

- When we need to retrieve the current date in the code, we always have to use `DateTime.UtcNow` instead of `DateTime.Now`

- Client applications must know that they will receive the date in UTC format and act accordingly, for example, invoking the `ToLocalTime()` method

In this way, the minimal API is truly globalized and can work with any time zone; without having to worry about explicit conversion, all times input or output will be always in UTC, so it will be much easier to handle them.

Summary

Developing minimal APIs with globalization and localization support in mind is fundamental in an interconnected world. ASP.NET Core includes all the features needed to create services that can react to the culture of the user and provide translations based on the request language: the usage of localization middleware, resource files, and custom validation messages allows the creation of services that can support virtually every culture. We have also talked about the globalization-related problems that could arise when working with different time zones and shown how to solve it using the centralized UTC date time format so that our APIs can seamlessly work irrespective of the geographic location and time zone of clients.

In *Chapter 10, Evaluating and Benchmarking the Performance of Minimal APIs*, we will talk about why minimal APIs were created and analyze the performance benefits of using minimal APIs over the classic controller-based approach.

10
Evaluating and Benchmarking the Performance of Minimal APIs

The purpose of this chapter is to understand one of the motivations for which the minimal APIs framework was created.

This chapter will provide some obvious data and examples of how you can measure the performance of an ASP.NET 6 application using the traditional approach as well as how you can measure the performance of an ASP.NET application using the minimal API approach.

Performance is key to any functioning application; however, very often it takes a back seat.

A performant and scalable application depends not only on our code but also on the development stack. Today, we have moved on from the .NET full framework and .NET Core to .NET and can start to appreciate the performance that the new .NET has achieved, version after version – not only with the introduction of new features and the clarity of the framework but also primarily because the framework has been completely rewritten and improved with many features that have made it fast and very competitive compared to other languages.

In this chapter, we will evaluate the performance of the minimal API by comparing its code with identical code that has been developed traditionally. We'll understand how to evaluate the performance of a web application, taking advantage of the **BenchmarkDotNet** framework, which can be useful in other application scenarios.

With minimal APIs, we have a new simplified framework that helps improve performance by leaving out some components that we take for granted with ASP.NET.

The themes we will touch on in this chapter are as follows:

- Improvements with minimal APIs

- Exploring performance with load tests

- Benchmarking minimal APIs with BenchmarkDotNet

Technical requirements

Many systems can help us test the performance of a framework.

We can measure how many requests per second one application can handle compared to another, assuming equal application load. In this case, we are talking about load testing.

To put the minimal APIs on the test bench, we need to install **k6**, the framework we will use for conducting our tests.

We will launch load testing on a Windows machine with only .NET applications running.

To install k6, you can do either one of the following:

- If you're using the *Chocolatey package manager* (`https://chocolatey.org/`), you can install the unofficial k6 package with the following command:

  ```
  choco install k6
  ```

- If you're using *Windows Package Manager* (`https://github.com/microsoft/winget-cli`), you can install the official package from the k6 manifests with this command:

  ```
  winget install k6
  ```

- You can also test your application published on the internet with Docker:

  ```
  docker pull loadimpact/k6
  ```

- Or as we did, we installed k6 on the Windows machine and launched everything from the command line. You can download k6 from this link: `https://dl.k6.io/msi/k6-latest-amd64.msi`.

In the final part of the chapter, we'll measure the duration of the HTTP method for making calls to the API.

We'll stand at the end of the system as if the API were a black box and measure the reaction time. BenchmarkDotNet is the tool we'll be using – to include it in our project, we need to reference its **NuGet** package:

```
dotnet add package BenchmarkDotNet
```

All the code samples in this chapter can be found in the GitHub repository for this book at the following link:

```
https://github.com/PacktPublishing/Minimal-APIs-in-ASP.NET-Core-6/
tree/main/Chapter10
```

Improvements with minimal APIs

Minimal APIs were designed not only to improve the performance of APIs but also for better code convenience and similarity to other languages to bring developers from other platforms closer. Performance has increased both from the point of view of the .NET framework, as each version has incredible improvements, as well as from the point of view of the simplification of the application pipeline. Let's see in detail what has not been ported and what improves the performance of this framework.

The minimal APIs execution pipeline omits the following features, which makes the framework lighter:

- Filters, such as `IAsyncAuthorizationFilter`, `IAsyncActionFilter`, `IAsyncExceptionFilter`, `IAsyncResultFilter`, and `IasyncResourceFilter`
- Model binding
- Binding for forms, such as `IFormFile`
- Built-in validation
- Formatters
- Content negotiations
- Some middleware
- View rendering
- JsonPatch
- OData
- API versioning

> **Performance Improvements in .NET 6**
>
> Version after version, .NET improves its performance. In the latest version of the framework, improvements made over previous versions have been reported. Here's where you can find a complete summary of what's new in .NET 6:
>
> `https://devblogs.microsoft.com/dotnet/performance-improvements-in-net-6/`

Exploring performance with load tests

How to estimate the performance of minimal APIs? There are many points of view to consider and in this chapter, we will try to address them from the point of view of the load they can support. We decided to adopt a tool – k6 – that performs load tests on a web application and tells us how many requests per second can a minimal API handle.

As described by its creators, k6 is an open source load testing tool that makes performance testing easy and productive for engineering teams. The tool is free, developer-centric, and extensible. Using k6, you can test the reliability and performance of your systems and catch performance regressions and problems earlier. This tool will help you to build resilient and performant applications that scale.

In our case, we would like to use the tool for performance evaluation and not for load testing. Many parameters should be considered during load testing, but we will only focus on the `http_reqs` index, which indicates how many requests have been handled correctly by the system.

We agree with the creators of k6 about the purpose of our test, namely *performance* and *synthetic monitoring*.

Use cases

k6 users are typically developers, QA engineers, SDETs, and SREs. They use k6 for testing the performance and reliability of APIs, microservices, and websites. Common k6 use cases include the following:

- **Load testing**: k6 is optimized for minimal resource consumption and designed for running high load tests (spike, stress, and soak tests).

- **Performance and synthetic monitoring**: With k6, you can run tests with a small load to continuously validate the performance and availability of your production environment.

- **Chaos and reliability testing**: k6 provides an extensible architecture. You can use k6 to simulate traffic as part of your chaos experiments or trigger them from your k6 tests.

However, we have to make several assumptions if we want to evaluate the application from the point of view just described. When a load test is performed, it is usually much more complex than the ones we will perform in this section. When an application is bombarded with requests, not all of them will be successful. We can say that the test passed successfully if a very small percentage of the responses failed. In particular, we usually consider 95 or 98 percentiles of outcomes as the statistic on which to derive the test numbers.

With this background, we can perform stepwise load testing as follows: in ramp up, the system will be concerned with running the **virtual user** (**VU**) load from 0 to 50 for about 15 seconds. Then, we will keep the number of users stable for 60 seconds, and finally, ramp down the load to zero virtual users for another 15 seconds.

Each newly written stage of the test is expressed in the JavaScript file in the *stages* section. Testing is therefore conducted under a simple empirical evaluation.

First, we create three types of responses, both for the ASP.NET Web API and minimal API:

- *Plain-text.*

- Very small *JSON* data against a call – the data is static and always the same.

- In the third response, we send JSON data with an HTTP POST method to the API. For the Web API, we check the *validation* of the object, and for the minimal API, since there is no validation, we return the object as received.

The following code will be used to compare the performance between the minimal API and the traditional approach:

Minimal API

```
app.MapGet("text-plain",() => Results.Content("response"))
.WithName("GetTextPlain");

app.MapPost("validations",(ValidationData validation) =>
Results.Ok(validation)).WithName("PostValidationData");

app.MapGet("jsons", () =>
    {
        var response = new[]
        {
            new PersonData { Name = "Andrea", Surname =
            "Tosato", BirthDate = new DateTime
            (2022, 01, 01) },
```

```
                new PersonData { Name = "Emanuele",
                Surname = "Bartolesi", BirthDate = new
                DateTime(2022, 01, 01) },
                new PersonData { Name = "Marco", Surname =
                "Minerva", BirthDate = new DateTime
                (2022, 01, 01) }
            };
            return Results.Ok(response);
        })
    .WithName("GetJsonData");
```

Traditional Approach

For the traditional approach, three distinct controllers have been designed as shown here:

```
[Route("text-plain")]
    [ApiController]
    public class TextPlainController : ControllerBase
    {
            [HttpGet]
            public IActionResult Get()
            {
                    return Content("response");
            }
    }
[Route("validations")]
    [ApiController]
    public class ValidationsController : ControllerBase
    {
            [HttpPost]
            public IActionResult Post(ValidationData data)
            {
                    return Ok(data);
            }
    }


    public class ValidationData
```

```
        {
                [Required]
                public int Id { get; set; }

                [Required]
                [StringLength(100)]
                public string Description { get; set; }
        }
[Route("jsons")]
[ApiController]
public class JsonsController : ControllerBase
{
        [HttpGet]
        public IActionResult Get()
        {
                var response = new[]
                {
                    new PersonData { Name = "Andrea", Surname =
                    "Tosato", BirthDate = new
                    DateTime(2022, 01, 01) },
                    new PersonData { Name = "Emanuele", Surname =
                    "Bartolesi", BirthDate = new
                    DateTime(2022, 01, 01) },
                    new PersonData { Name = "Marco", Surname =
                    "Minerva", BirthDate = new
                    DateTime(2022, 01, 01) }
                };
                return Ok(response);
        }
}

        public class PersonData
        {
                public string Name { get; set; }
                public string Surname { get; set; }
```

```
            public DateTime BirthDate { get; set; }
    }
```

In the next section, we will define an `options` object, where we are going to define the execution ramp described here. We define all clauses to consider the test satisfied. As the last step, we write the real test, which does nothing but call the HTTP endpoint using `GET` or `POST`, depending on the test.

Writing k6 tests

Let's create a test for each case scenario that we described in the previous section:

```
import http from "k6/http";
import { check } from "k6";

export let options = {
    summaryTrendStats: ["avg", "p(95)"],
    stages: [
            // Linearly ramp up from 1 to 50 VUs during 10
                seconds
                { target: 50, duration: "10s" },
            // Hold at 50 VUs for the next 1 minute
                { target: 50, duration: "1m" },
            // Linearly ramp down from 50 to 0 VUs over the
                last 15 seconds
                { target: 0, duration: "15s" }
    ],
    thresholds: {
            // We want the 95th percentile of all HTTP
                request durations to be less than 500ms
                "http_req_duration": ["p(95)<500"],
            // Thresholds based on the custom metric we
                defined and use to track application failures
                "check_failure_rate": [
            // Global failure rate should be less than 1%
                "rate<0.01",
            // Abort the test early if it climbs over 5%
                { threshold: "rate<=0.05", abortOnFail: true },
            ],
```

```
    },
};

export default function () {
    // execute http get call
    let response = http.get("http://localhost:7060/jsons");
    // check() returns false if any of the specified
       conditions fail
    check(response, {
        "status is 200": (r) => r.status === 200,
    });
}
```

In the preceding JavaScript file, we wrote the test using k6 syntax. We have defined the options, such as the evaluation threshold of the test, the parameters to be measured, and the stages that the test should simulate. Once we have defined the options of the test, we just have to write the code to call the APIs that interest us – in our case, we have defined three tests to call the three endpoints that we want to evaluate.

Running a k6 performance test

Now that we have written the code to test the performance, let's run the test and generate the statistics of the tests.

We will report all the general statistics of the collected tests:

1. First, we need to start the web applications to run the load test. Let's start with both the ASP.NET Web API application and the minimal API application. We expose the URLs, both the HTTPS and HTTP protocols.

2. Move the shell to the root folder and run the following two commands in two different shells:

```
dotnet .\MinimalAPI.Sample\bin\Release\net6.0\MinimalAPI.
Sample.dll --urls=https://localhost:7059/;http://
localhost:7060/

dotnet .\ControllerAPI.Sample\bin\Release\
net6.0\ControllerAPI.Sample.dll --urls="https://
localhost:7149/;http://localhost:7150/"
```

3.   Now, we just have to run the three test files for each project.

   -   This one is for the controller-based Web API:

```
k6 run .\K6\Controllers\json.js --summary-export=.\K6\
results\controller-json.json
```

   -   This one is for the minimal API:

```
k6 run .\K6\Minimal\json.js --summary-export=.\K6\
results\minimal-json.json
```

Here are the results.

For the test in traditional development mode with a plain-text content type, the number of requests served per second is 1,547:

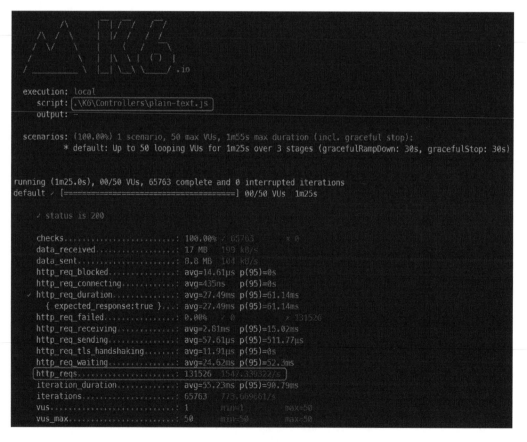

Figure 10.1 – The load test for a controller-based API and plain text

For the test in traditional development mode with a `json` content type, the number of requests served per second is 1,614:

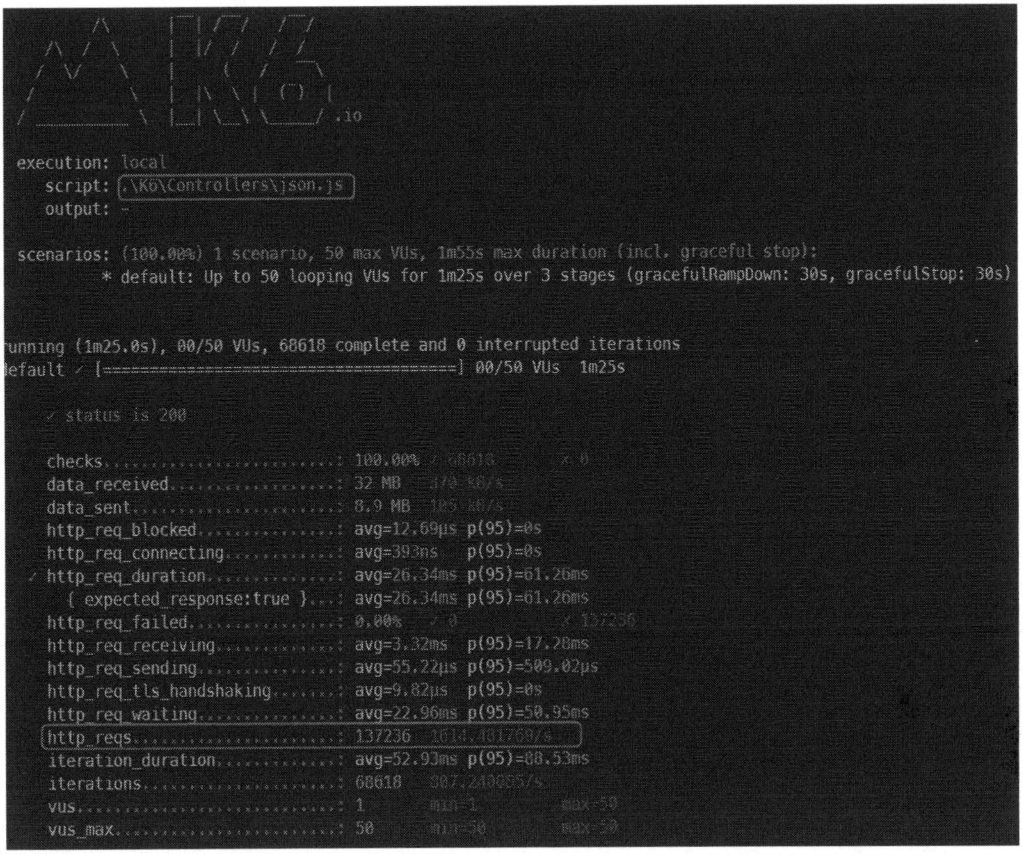

Figure 10.2 – The load test for a controller-based API and JSON result

For the test in traditional development mode with a json content type and model validation, the number of requests served per second is 1,602:

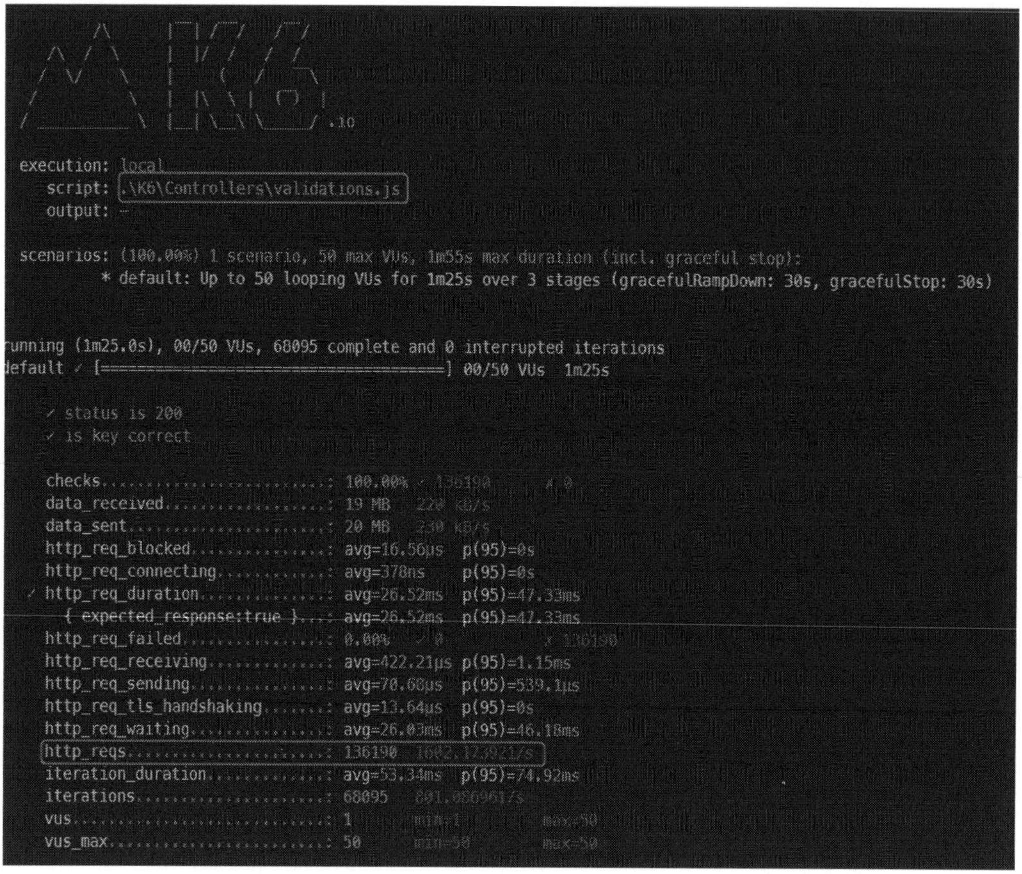

Figure 10.3 – The load test for a controller-based API and validation payload

For the test in minimal API development mode with a `plain-text` content type, the number of requests served per second is 2,285:

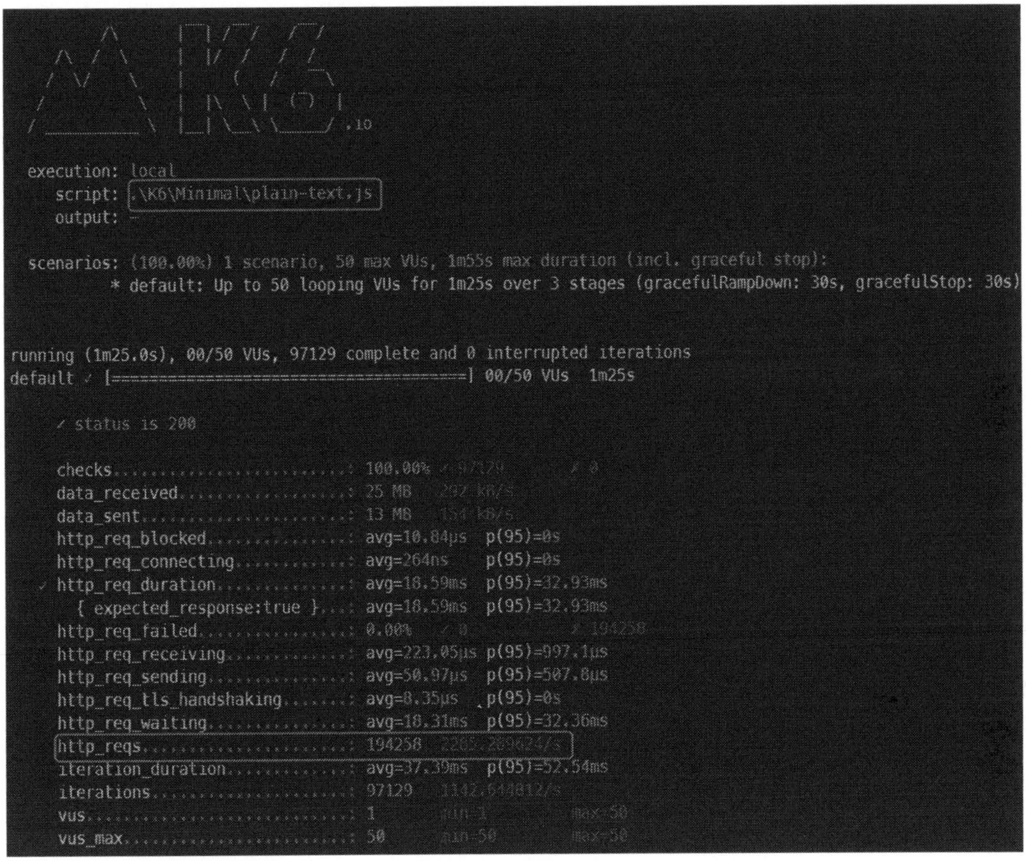

Figure 10.4 – The load test for a minimal API and plain text

For the test in minimal API development mode with a `json` content type, the number of requests served per second is 2,030:

```
         /\      |‾‾| /‾‾/  /‾‾/
    /\  /  \     |  |/  /  /  /
   /  \/    \    |     (  /   ‾‾\
  /          \   |  |\  \ |  (‾)  |
 / _____ \  |__| \__\ \_____/ .io

  execution: local
     script: .\K6\Minimal\json.js
     output: -

  scenarios: (100.00%) 1 scenario, 50 max VUs, 1m55s max duration (incl. graceful stop):
           * default: Up to 50 looping VUs for 1m25s over 3 stages (gracefulRampDown: 30s, gracefulStop: 30s)


running (1m25.0s), 00/50 VUs, 86315 complete and 0 interrupted iterations
default ✓ [======================================] 00/50 VUs  1m25s

     ✓ status is 200

     checks.........................: 100.00% ✓ 86315        ✗ 0
     data_received..................: 40 MB   465 kB/s
     data_sent......................: 11 MB   131 kB/s
     http_req_blocked...............: avg=10.46µs  p(95)=0s
     http_req_connecting............: avg=272ns    p(95)=0s
   ✓ http_req_duration..............: avg=20.93ms  p(95)=49.22ms
       { expected_response:true }...: avg=20.93ms  p(95)=49.22ms
     http_req_failed................: 0.00%   ✓ 0           ✗ 172630
     http_req_receiving.............: avg=1.05ms   p(95)=7.43ms
     http_req_sending...............: avg=55.24µs  p(95)=509.75µs
     http_req_tls_handshaking.......: avg=7.82µs   p(95)=0s
     http_req_waiting...............: avg=19.81ms  p(95)=45.2ms
     http_reqs......................: 172630  2030.638024/s
     iteration_duration.............: avg=42.06ms  p(95)=77.14ms
     iterations.....................: 86315   1015.319012/s
     vus............................: 1       min=1         max=50
     vus_max........................: 50      min=50        max=50
```

Figure 10.5 – The load test for a minimal API and JSON result

For the test in minimal API development mode with a json content type with model validation, the number of requests served per second is 2,070:

```
       /\      |‾‾|  /‾‾/  /‾‾/
      /\ /\    |  |_/  /  /  /
     /  \/  \  |      |  /  ‾‾\
    /          \ |  |‾\  \ |  (_)  |
   /  _____  \ |__| \__\ \_____/ .io

 execution: local
    script: .\K6\Minimal\validations.js
    output: -

 scenarios: (100.00%) 1 scenario, 50 max VUs, 1m55s max duration (incl. graceful stop):
          * default: Up to 50 looping VUs for 1m25s over 3 stages (gracefulRampDown: 30s, gracefulStop: 30s)

 running (1m25.0s), 00/50 VUs, 87982 complete and 0 interrupted iterations
 default ✓ [======================================] 00/50 VUs  1m25s

      ✓ status is 200
      ✓ is key correct

      checks.........................: 100.00% ✓ 175964      ✗ 0
      data_received..................: 24 MB   284 kB/s
      data_sent......................: 25 MB   296 kB/s
      http_req_blocked...............: avg=10.15µs p(95)=0s
      http_req_connecting............: avg=287ns   p(95)=0s
    ✓ http_req_duration..............: avg=20.5ms  p(95)=53.97ms
        { expected_response:true }...: avg=20.5ms  p(95)=53.97ms
      http_req_failed................: 0.00%   ✓ 0          ✗ 175964
      http_req_receiving.............: avg=1.37ms  p(95)=9.19ms
      http_req_sending...............: avg=70.44µs p(95)=537.78µs
      http_req_tls_handshaking.......: avg=7.5µs   p(95)=0s
      http_req_waiting...............: avg=19.05ms p(95)=48.35ms
      http_reqs......................: 175964  2070.117671/s
      iteration_duration.............: avg=41.28ms p(95)=81.37ms
      iterations.....................: 87982   1035.058785/s
      vus............................: 1       min=1        max=50
      vus_max........................: 50      min=50       max=50
```

Figure 10.6 – The load test for a minimal API and no validation payload

In the following image, we show a comparison of the three tested functionalities, reporting the number of requests served with the same functionality:

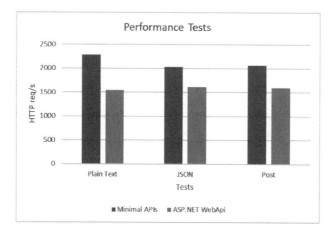

Figure 10.7 – The performance results

As we might have expected, minimal APIs are much faster than controller-based web APIs.

The difference is approximately 30%, and that's no small feat.

Obviously, as previously mentioned, minimal APIs have features missing in order to optimize performance, the most striking being data validation.

In the example, the payload is very small, and the differences are not very noticeable.

As the payload and validation rules grow, the difference in speed between the two frameworks will only increase.

We have seen how to measure performance with a load testing tool and then evaluate how many requests it can serve per second with the same number of machines and users connected.

We can also use other tools to understand how minimal APIs have had a strong positive impact on performance.

Benchmarking minimal APIs with BenchmarkDotNet

BenchmarkDotNet is a framework that allows you to measure written code and compare performance between libraries written in different versions or compiled with different .NET frameworks.

This tool is used for calculating the time taken for the execution of a task, the memory used, and many other parameters.

Our case is a very simple scenario. We want to compare the response times of two applications written to the same version of the .NET Framework.

How do we perform this comparison? We take an `HttpClient` object and start calling the methods that we have also defined for the load testing case.

We will therefore obtain a comparison between two methods that exploit the same `HttpClient` object and recall methods with the same functionality, but one is written with the ASP.NET Web API and the traditional controllers, while the other is written using minimal APIs.

BenchmarkDotNet helps you to transform methods into benchmarks, track their performance, and share reproducible measurement experiments.

Under the hood, it performs a lot of magic that guarantees reliable and precise results thanks to the perfolizer statistical engine. BenchmarkDotNet protects you from popular benchmarking mistakes and warns you if something is wrong with your benchmark design or obtained measurements. The library has been adopted by over 6,800 projects, including .NET Runtime, and is supported by the .NET Foundation (`https://benchmarkdotnet.org/`).

Running BenchmarkDotNet

We will write a class that represents all the methods for calling the APIs of the two web applications. Let's make the most of the startup feature and prepare the objects we will send via POST. The function marked as `[GlobalSetup]` is not computed during runtime, and this helps us calculate exactly how long it takes between the call and the response from the web application:

1. Register all the classes in `Program.cs` that implement BenchmarkDotNet:

    ```
    BenchmarkSwitcher.FromAssembly(typeof(Program).Assembly).
    Run(args);
    ```

    In the preceding snippet, we have registered the current assembly that implements all the functions that will be needed to be evaluated in the performance calculation. The methods marked with `[Benchmark]` will be executed over and over again to establish the average execution time.

2. The application must be compiled on release and possibly within the production environment:

    ```
    namespace DotNetBenchmarkRunners
    {
        [SimpleJob(RuntimeMoniker.Net60, baseline: true)]
        [JsonExporter]
        public class Performances
        {
            private readonly HttpClient clientMinimal =
            new HttpClient();
            private readonly HttpClient
            clientControllers = new HttpClient();
    ```

```csharp
private readonly ValidationData data = new
ValidationData()
{
    Id = 1,
    Description = "Performance"
};

[GlobalSetup]
public void Setup()
{
    clientMinimal.BaseAddress = new
    Uri("https://localhost:7059");
    clientControllers.BaseAddress = new
    Uri("https://localhost:7149");
}

[Benchmark]
public async Task Minimal_Json_Get() =>
await clientMinimal.GetAsync("/jsons");

[Benchmark]
public async Task Controller_Json_Get() =>
await clientControllers.GetAsync("/jsons");

[Benchmark]
public async Task Minimal_TextPlain_Get()
=> await clientMinimal.
GetAsync("/text-plain");

[Benchmark]
public async Task
Controller_TextPlain_Get() => await
clientControllers.GetAsync("/text-plain");

[Benchmark]
public async Task Minimal_Validation_Post()
```

```
        => await clientMinimal.
        PostAsJsonAsync("/validations", data);



        [Benchmark]
        public async Task
        Controller_Validation_Post() => await
        clientControllers.
        PostAsJsonAsync("/validations", data);
    }

    public class ValidationData
    {
        public int Id { get; set; }
        public string Description { get; set; }
    }
}
```

3.   Before launching the benchmark application, launch the web applications:

Minimal API application

```
dotnet .\MinimalAPI.Sample\bin\Release\net6.0\MinimalAPI.
Sample.dll --urls="https://localhost:7059/;http://
localhost:7060/"
```

Controller-based application

```
dotnet .\ControllerAPI.Sample\bin\Release\
net6.0\ControllerAPI.Sample.dll --urls=https://
localhost:7149/;http://localhost:7150/
```

By launching these applications, various steps will be performed and a summary report will
be extracted with the timelines that we report here:

```
dotnet .\DotNetBenchmarkRunners\bin\Release\net6.0\
DotNetBenchmarkRunners.dll --filter *
```

For each method performed, the average value or the average execution time is reported.

Method	Mean	Error	StdDev	Ratio
Minimal_Json_Get	545.0 µs	5.23 µs	4.89 µs	1.00
Controller_Json_Get	840.1 µs	13.29 µs	11.78 µs	1.00
Minimal_TextPlain_Get	596.8 µs	3.84 µs	3.20 µs	1.00
Controller_TextPlain_Get	891.7 µs	7.50 µs	9.21 µs	1.00
Minimal_Validation_Post	596.8 µs	5.95 µs	5.28 µs	1.00
Controller_Validation_Post	905.6 µs	5.18 µs	4.59 µs	1.00

Table 10.1 – Benchmark HTTP requests for minimal APIs and controllers

In the following table, **Error** denotes how much the average value may vary due to a measurement error. Finally, the standard deviation (**StdDev**) indicates the deviation from the mean value. The times are given in **µs** and are therefore very small to measure empirically if not with instruments with that just exposed.

Summary

In the chapter, we compared the performance of minimal APIs with that of the traditional approach by using two very different methods.

Minimal APIs were not designed for performance alone and evaluating them solely on that basis is a poor starting point.

Table 10.1 indicates that there are a lot of differences between the responses of minimal APIs and that of traditional ASP.NET Web API applications.

The tests were conducted on the same machine with the same resources. We found that minimal APIs performed about 30% better than the traditional framework.

We have learned about how to measure the speed of our applications – this can be useful for understanding whether the application will hold the load and what response time it can offer. We can also leverage this on small portions of critical code.

As a final note, the applications tested were practically bare bones. The validation part that should be evaluated in the ASP.NET Web API application is almost irrelevant since there are only two fields to consider. The gap between the two frameworks increases as the number of components that have been eliminated in the minimal APIs that we have already described increases.

Index

Symbols

A

B

Packt.com

Subscribe to our online digital library for full access to over 7,000 books and videos, as well as industry leading tools to help you plan your personal development and advance your career. For more information, please visit our website.

Why subscribe?

- Spend less time learning and more time coding with practical eBooks and Videos from over 4,000 industry professionals
- Improve your learning with Skill Plans built especially for you
- Get a free eBook or video every month
- Fully searchable for easy access to vital information
- Copy and paste, print, and bookmark content

Did you know that Packt offers eBook versions of every book published, with PDF and ePub files available? You can upgrade to the eBook version at packt.com and as a print book customer, you are entitled to a discount on the eBook copy. Get in touch with us at customercare@packtpub.com for more details.

At www.packt.com, you can also read a collection of free technical articles, sign up for a range of free newsletters, and receive exclusive discounts and offers on Packt books and eBooks.

Other Books You May Enjoy

If you enjoyed this book, you may be interested in these other books by Packt:

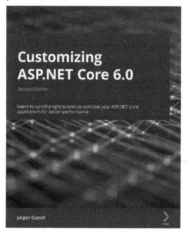

Customizing ASP.NET Core 6.0 - Second Edition

Jürgen Gutsch

ISBN: 978-1-80323-360-4

- Explore various application configurations and providers in ASP.NET Core 6
- Enable and work with caches to improve the performance of your application
- Understand dependency injection in .NET and learn how to add third-party DI containers
- Discover the concept of middleware and write your middleware for ASP.NET Core apps
- Create various API output formats in your API-driven projects
- Get familiar with different hosting models for your ASP.NET Core app

ASP.NET Core 6 and Angular - Fifth Edition

Valerio De Sanctis

ISBN: 978-1-80323-970-5

- Use the new Visual Studio Standalone TypeScript Angular template
- Implement and consume a Web API interface with ASP.NET Core
- Set up an SQL database server using a local instance or a cloud datastore
- Perform C# and TypeScript debugging using Visual Studio 2022
- Create TDD and BDD unit tests using xUnit, Jasmine, and Karma
- Perform DBMS structured logging using providers such as SeriLog
- Deploy web apps to Azure App Service using IIS, Kestrel, and NGINX
- Learn to develop fast and flexible Web APIs using GraphQL
- Add real-time capabilities to Angular apps with ASP.NET Core SignalR

Packt is searching for authors like you

If you're interested in becoming an author for Packt, please visit `authors.packtpub.com` and apply today. We have worked with thousands of developers and tech professionals, just like you, to help them share their insight with the global tech community. You can make a general application, apply for a specific hot topic that we are recruiting an author for, or submit your own idea.

Hi!

We are Andrea Tosato, Marco Minerva, and Emanuele Bartolesi authors of *Mastering Minimal APIs in ASP.NET Core*. We really hope you enjoyed reading this book and found it useful for increasing your productivity and efficiency in ASP.NET Core.

It would really help us (and other potential readers!) if you could leave a review on Amazon sharing your thoughts on *Mastering Minimal APIs in ASP.NET Core*.

Go to the link below or scan the QR code to leave your review:

`https://packt.link/r/1803237821`

Your review will help us to understand what's worked well in this book, and what could be improved upon for future editions, so it really is appreciated.

Best Wishes,

Andrea Tosato

Marco Minerva

Emanuele Bartolesi

Made in United States
Orlando, FL
26 January 2023

29076602R00133